A Jewish Dialectic

A
JEWISH
DIALECTIC

HARRY Z. SKY

Quiet Waters Publications
Bolivar, Missouri
2011

Copyright ©2011 by Harry Sky. All rights reserved. No part of this book may be used or reproduced in any manner without written permission, except in the case of brief quotations embodied in critical articles and reviews.

Quiet Waters Publications
P.O. Box 34, Bolivar MO 65613-0034.
Email: QWP@usa.net.

For prices and order information visit:
www.quietwaterspub.com

ISBN 978-1-931475-53-2
Library of Congress Control Number: 2011936365

DEDICATION

In this book, my thoughts are a summation and a culmination of my lifelong beliefs.

I dedicate this book to my family and my late wives: Ruth Helen Levinson and Helene Gerstein; and my children Rina, Uri, and Ari and their families.

In the latter part of my life, I had the privilege of associating with Bernard Osher. Thanks to his generosity and vision, we can say life for us older people has been enriched.

I want to thank my secretary, Carol Rauch, for her editorial guidance.

Above all, I am grateful for the friendship of Dr. David Trobisch and his deep spiritual sensitivity.

I'VE ALWAYS FELT THAT IN THE CHAOS OF LIFE SEEDS ARE TO BE FOUND FOR NEW AND INTERESTING DEVELOPMENTS. WE ARE ALWAYS IN A STATE OF BECOMING; WE ARE NEVER IN A STATE OF ARRIVAL.

I

I've been wondering for many years what prompted the definitive statements of the Tanach. It's very easy, in fact almost effortless, to say, "God told me so." Why did He speak to you and no one else? Wouldn't it be better to say most of these statements were attempts to bring about some civilized society among Jews and the proof was "God told me so." If you didn't have rules and regulations pertaining to the worth of human life, what would prompt people to abstain from violence? It's much easier to accept the verse, "uproot the evil among you." If I have a bat in my hand or, in later times, bows and arrows, spears, and of late, guns, and engage their power, it's a natural thing to use that power. We may say it's beyond reason, but it's not beyond nature.

Some realized: If you're going to have any kind of society, the society needs brakes, some force that says "stop" when you're ready to destroy. I think that's the beginning of the dialectic.

Read carefully the Cain and Abel story and think about the passage where God says to Cain, "Misdeeds lurk at your door enticing you and seducing you." You can, if you want to, say "no thanks" and follow another path. In other words, it's in our power as humans to put a halt to the negative and the destructive in human society.

From my reading of the Hebrew Bible, known as the *Tanach*, the human is God's representative on Earth who has been given the task of making sure that the Earth stays whole and that its potential is realized. It's a simple statement, but its ramifications go deeply into the very psyche of the Human. To us, if we accept this Biblical notion as reality and not as the figment of someone's imagination, we humans have tremendous power. But, as the voice of Adonai says to Cain, the opportunity for going one way or another lurks at *your* very door. The choice is yours. All of Scripture is but an example of this thesis applied.

We plan in this composition to address our proposition and try bit by bit to show its application and its success or failure.

Let us begin at the beginning. According to our sages, we should read the first verse in Genesis, or as it is known in Hebrew, *B'rayshit*, as follows: "With *Rayshit* (another word for Torah), God formed or created the Universe—the skies above and the earth below." Now, assuming there was a document prior to Creation that the Creator consulted, we are faced with the possibility that this document was a summary of *all other attempts* at creation prior to the one in which we are living. It can also be Scripture's way of dealing with DNA. If this be true, then the notion that this Universe, in which we find ourselves, *is the Creation* is open to question. This *Rayshit* or document of past experiences is, therefore, greater than the Torah or the Tanach itself.

There were and are many fundamentalists among our Jewish people who shun such doctrines. They said the *Torah* or the Tanach which we now possess comes directly from God. The Torah especially was presented to our ancestors at Mt. Sinai after their release from slavery/serfdom in Egypt. Many questions arise in our mind when we assert this *fact*. What shall we do with the *Midrash* that says there were many creations prior to this one? Why must we follow the rationalists' tradition that always said such *Midrashim* are sacrilegious? They are not to be taken as the true words of our living tradition. Some say they are in a category known as *"Midrash Pelie,"* strange Midrashim. Yet there is another tradition which we hear again and again in Jewish studies: "I have gained wisdom from all my teachers," whether from the tradition or from elsewhere. Throughout the rabbinic literature, such Midrashim are cited and often times used as positive proof for a thought or a tradition.

In our studies, we have found time and again thoughts, deeds, approaches which remind us of our tradition. We know wherever we Jews have been, we have become acculturated and absorbed, and sometimes we redefined the traditions of our guest hosts. We cannot at any point say this or that is wholly Jewish. Just as we cannot say of any human that his or her DNA is solely his own and nowhere in this world can a duplicate be found.

Let us return to Rayshit. Let us continue our translation. With Rayshit, *Elohim* (which is a collective name for all the God forces that exist in this universe) created or formed the upper spheres known as *shamayim*, heaven or sky, and the lower spheres known as *erets*, earth, or better still, *terra firma*. We are not told what energies, what force, what physical manifestations occurred at that moment. This statement is quite clear: It happened.

For us to completely understand what "Adonai asks of us," we have to go behind the text. One can't expect *Adonai* to ask of a human that which is impossible. For many, many millenia, the accepted notion was "to the victor belongs the spoils," "might makes right," the conqueror is not bound by restraints. If he has conquered "fairly and squarely," then whatever is there belongs to him or her. Along comes the Biblical tradition and says, nope, that's not the way it works. You have to choose between one way and another. The important thing is you must always ask yourself the question, what will assure human survival? What will aid the earth and the fullness thereof in its desire to produce all that is needed for human survival?

If you read the Book of *B'Rayshit* (Genesis) carefully, you will note that the early chapters are examples of failed human endeavors. Immediately after the story of Noah and the ark, or better still, the Great Flood, the Creator states that there is an evil streak in the Human. He is not *like us*. He is not the perfect imitation of the Godly. He is not an *Adonai, Jr.* But, says the Creator, even so, I will never allow for the utter destruction of the Universe and the Human.

II

This being so, accepting this promise, I have asked many times that if the Universe will never be totally destroyed, why can't we have a situation where no destruction will ensue? Why can't we humans come up with a formula which will assure non-destruction, a formula that will provide for the feeding of all and make the great dream of each one living under his own vine tree a reality? What stands in the way? Part of the promise that the Universe will never be completely destroyed is the assumption that on the whole, we humans will make the correct choices and we won't be the avengers and destroyers. In fact, we'll be the builders and the mergers. When two people agree, shake hands, draw up documents, and with all honesty and integrity follow the road of cooperation, the foundations needed for survival will be strengthened. The text tells us if Adonai is involved in this undertaking. In other words, if we are prompted by high spiritual designs, disintegration will not occur. When the honest in heart, the committed in faith, the hopeful in belief, and the peace-pursuers in fact take over, nothing but good can be its result.

Any student of Jewish tradition who takes to heart the Jewish rule of human life will realize quite early there is something divine within us. Call it *soul*. Call it *breath*. Call it *the God-presence itself*, or call it *goodness*. It's that something that distinguishes us from the rest of Creation. We have everything that the plants have, the fish and the fowl, but we have that little extra piece articulated by the Creator at the time of human creation (according to the text) that describes us as the divine replica created to be the caretakers of this Universe. According to Genesis, the Creator said, "Let us make a being like Ourself." The Human is that being. The Human contains within itself that spark, that creative impulse we normally define as the *Divine*. The kabbalists—the Jewish mystics—call it the *Tov*, the essential goodness that exists in every being. How can we be assured of the validity of this proposition? It's basically a mystical, somewhat poetic notion, not open to scientific proof. It's true, various thinkers have come close to describing it in the fullest way, yet, they have missed the boat. They use as their measure the canons of human science. This divinity, the spirit of which we speak, is of an energy stream separate from the energy that assures us humans life. The divine energy stream never ends. Human energy does. The divine stream can be sensed in our DNA.

In Jewish tradition, the memorial prayer (El Malay Rachamim) is recited at a funeral service, the notion being that the *Neshama*, the divine presence that is within us, is being gathered into the divine presence that has always existed. In other words, the initial divine breath returns to its source.

If a true Jewish theology were to be written, it would say to us that our purpose as humans is to act as the Creator's deputy watching over the well-being of the Creator's creation, whether it be in the fields, in the waters, in the sky, whether it be vegetation, fish and fowl, cattle, birds, what have you. In fact, if you read the mystical literature, it includes anything and everything that has a spark of life, from the initial one-celled amoeba to the multi-celled human.

Assuming the correctness of this proposition, we may therefore say the purpose of Jewish faith and theology is forever to mend whatever is broken in this universe—God's creation. If you read carefully that awesome work known as the *Tanya*, you sense these beliefs. I suspect I arrived at them very early in life. My father, through his family, had very deep roots in all that the Tanya taught. The author of the Tanya was Rabbi Shneur Zalman of Ladi in the Baltic area. Rabbi Shneur Zalman said, "There is no perfect human-being." There are people who are close to perfection, but none who are completely so. He taught that everyone follows a middle path between light and darkness, good and evil. He called this middle path the *Way of the Middle*, or in Hebrew, *Derech Haemtzai*. I sensed quite early in life that in most situations, to play it safe, follow the middle path. Don't be driven to be on top of the mountain or, as the children say, the "king of the mountain." Let your friendships be many. May they include the wise and the simple, the wealthy and the poor. For basically, they all possess an inherent goodness. They came into life with it. It is called in Hebrew, *Tov*. Our life's journey is the pursuit of the Tov within ourselves and the Tov within the rest of Creation. With patience, animal trainers have taught us that the ferocious can be converted to the tame.

If we use this measure—the pursuit of the *Tov*, we would avoid the various pitfalls of modern life. It seems in our times success is measured not by Tov—goodness, kindness, compassion, charity, love, togetherness, oneness—but by one's acquisitive skills. If I hit on a plan which goes beyond the norm and the established and I make a "killing," I'm considered a cultural hero. Even if I break the law, my audacity comes to my defense; and few and far between are those judges who ignore the audacious. We look for audacity in our children. We want them to be teen leaders. We guide them onto paths of achievement and judge them by it. Seldom is the conversation around the dinner table focused on acts of human kindness and compassion, but rather on acts of "success."

Of late, I have felt as if we are in a moment of history where the Creation process has to be triggered again. Since Roman times there have been historic moments. When the great economic meltdown of 2008 took place and all the scandals and the dishonest acts were revealed, I had the feeling that the Biblical verse, "the Earth was filled with violence and destructiveness," is true again. I had images, dreams, and moments of active imagination pounding in the recesses of my mind and psyche. I don't think we are in a period when sermons from pulpits, cajoling or harassing, soothing or making one feel good, can turn things around. Carl Jung once said the healing of the world has to take place in every one of us. I agree.

A story is told of the Rabbi Memel who greeted everyone, friend and foe alike, with a warm "Good morning." When he was taken and brought to a concentration camp, the Sudeten

German guard recognized the rabbi and said, "Guten Morgen Herr Rabbiner" and put him into the camp of the workers. He watched over him and assured his survival. I once told this story to a young group of children. One of them said to me, "Rabbi, whenever you use the word 'good,' something good will happen." How true. The good in us awaits us, hoping it can be awakened and become part of our daily routine.

III

Jewish tradition has never accepted a pessimistic view of the Human. Nowhere are we taught the Human is eternally damned. Nor do we find texts which lead us to believe our salvation is in someone else's hands, not our own. In fact, the whole concept of *Mitzvot* (divine connections) assumes the inner power of such deeds. In fact, some of our mystics taught whenever a *mitzvah* is performed, some broken aspect of the world is healed. We are so imbibed with the notion of a mitzvah's power that we have been taught the performing of one mitzvah will almost automatically lead to another. The road to goodness is not paved with good intentions, but rather it is a natural road waiting for those who want to traverse it. The goodness within us is oftentimes tucked away in an unfamiliar corner. We have to become investigators of these corners, hoping to find the elusive goodness.

Since the journey towards goodness is a lifetime affair, we must necessarily expect many detours, enticements, assurances of various kinds of glories, seductive words and deeds. In short, this journey is a personal journey. A mitzvah takes root only when it is accompanied by good and honest intentions. Our sages taught us, be wary of the one who carries the history of his *good deeds* on his sleeves. Be wary of the boaster and the person trapped in self-glorification. By such attitudes, he has lessened the possibility of his mitzvot being true mitzvot. True mitzvot help mend the tears of this world.

What are these tears? When a community is built on selfishness, it is torn and riven, never allowing space for the innate goodness that is within us.

Rabbi Shneur Zalman whom we quoted earlier seldom scolded anyone. He felt all of us in one way or another are seeking the good. He also said all of us, because of our human frailties, sometimes embark on the wrong paths. But, said he, even the prisoner, separated from the rest of the world, will in a moment of meditation find his own inner goodness and light and attempt to follow it.

IV

Recently it occurred to us that the most profound thinker of our times (by that I mean from the sixteenth century onwards) was Rabbi Shneur Zalman of Ladi. Not only was he a learned Jew, but much of his writings anticipated the theories of modern depth psychology. Jung's theory of the Self could easily be Shneur Zalman's theory of Neshama. The Self, I would say, is, in Jung's eyes, that part of the human situation or the human-being which is as old as the human species itself. Shneur Zalman would say that the breath (Neshama) of each person can be traced back to that moment when God, the Creator, placed within the Human a part of God's self. Furthermore, Shneur Zalman refused to label the Human in terms of Tsadik (totally righteous) and Rasha (totally evil). As we said earlier, at no time is the Human totally one or the other. We run the gamut. The same Human has the *Tov*, the good, in him or her as he or she has the *Rah*, the evil, in him- or herself. Assuming the correctness of this insight and further assuming the reality of the spiritual journey upon which all humans are embarked, then we—who want the great dream of all the "people of the spirit"—will someday experience it. The great Rabbi, Shneur Zalman, said that even in a moment of total darkness/evil, there is the other side.

Having all this information and feelings and insights as to what the great thinkers are trying to tell us, how can we possibly hope to be of this world, to be part of human evolution, and to avoid the spiritual questions?

Martin Buber gathered together many of the Hasidic tales. These tales spoke constantly of the awareness and the nearness of God. They had many names for God. They seldom used the word, Adonai, but rather spoke of *Hashem*, which means "the One of Whom we speak but Whose name we never say." In these stories, you sense the closeness of the Human and Hashem. The community that nurtured these stories said in their ditties, "Hashem is all over." Wherever you turn, you will find Hashem. Hashem may not answer you immediately, but ultimately the answers to your questions will arrive. To be a follower of Hashem is a burdensome task. Many of us have some profound questions. In every generation we ask "Hashem, where are You?" Even though the question may seem skeptical, it insists on the reality of Hashem. The question of "Hashem, where are You," comes from our experience. If Hashem is all over, if His presence can be found in every corner of the Universe, then we must ask: Where were you when we needed you? The Hassid will insist that Death is not a final answer to anything. Death is only a passageway. Death, burial, oblivion, nothingness, being gone, seems to say to us, "Okay. What you've known till now as life has ended. But life itself continues in another way." The same thing is said by the Hassid when he sees another human who is not acting in the way of Tov or goodness and seems to be embarked on a road that contradicts goodness. The Hassid will tell you *that* human is never a total loss, just someone who has lost his way.

V

Many years ago, I delivered a Lenten lecture before a non-Jewish group. It was titled, "The Faith we Live By." Some proper ladies sitting in the audience wondered: What faith do the Jews possess? To them, the only proper faith was the faith of their fathers. Many of these proper ladies felt called to serve as missionaries to various parts of the world hoping to share the faith of their fathers with people who lived otherwise. In the early days of my Rabbinate, from 1951-1961 (the year I arrived in Portland Maine), I spoke to many non-Jewish groups. My task, my mission, was to share with others what we believed. I wasn't a missionary; I never said to anyone, "If you don't believe as I do, you will be damned to Hell." I believed deeply in Hashem (God) and never felt totally abandoned. Maybe neglected, but not abandoned. God may be hidden, as Abraham Joshua Heschel once said, but Hashem has never left us. Even in the darkest moments of our various exiles, He has never left us. Thus in a moment of loneliness, when you or I or anyone feel like a stray flower in the unplowed field, we need not throw up our hands in despair. The secure child knows, Papa's or Mama's absence does not mean Papa or Mama will never be back. He's absent, but never gone forever.

Let us return to the creation story. It really is a guide for life. First, it assures us that within ourselves there is a divine aspect. Hashem lives in us. And the signature of his presence is the bit of *tov*—goodness that lies within us. When we Jews look at the creation story, we see it as a source of potential. Some of our detractors see it as the first example of disobedience. When I read the creation story, I am on Adam's side. His Father—Hashem—Mr.

Perfect—is a mythic being. None like him ever existed. If you read the creation story, you know that this is not Hashem or God's first attempt at creation. There were many civilizations prior to this one. Every part of Adam, which was the end product of all that had been previously created, said to himself, "This Being, Hashem, is a new force in this Universe. This Being believes in us Humans. This Being says we have great potential, possibly even achieving the highest heights. Why does he believe in us? What does he see in us? What has he instilled in us that's new, that's unique, that can't be found in any of the previous creations?" First, the desire for power, sometimes destruction, isn't a natural phenomenon. We possess a breath, or better still, a *neshama*, a soul, that separates us from all other creations. This soul yearns to be forever at Hashem's side, unlike some of the other creations.

We can never dismiss Hashem's existence. As the Biblical story tells us, Hashem is the One who brought to fruition what we know today as human society. There are many who would like to believe that the act of creation was a one-time affair, that Hashem did what he had to do, and then crawled back into his own cave, never to be seen or to be heard of again. I, for one, dismiss such notions.

I don't accept death as a word for oblivion. In fact, the Hebrew word for death is *Mavet*. According to Brown Driver Brigg's lexicon, the word Mavet equals *Death*. Its opposite is *Life*, implying that the state of Death is beyond the state of Life. That being so, it never signifies the total end of anything, but rather a state of something. If that be the case, then Death is just a period of existence and not a replacement of existence. Can it be that our tradition is trying to tell us that what we call *Death* is just another level of existence? It may not be a replacement of existence. Continuing with that train of thought, might we not say that when Death occurs, the body ceases to function in its normal way? Whatever has accrued or been acquired by the body during its period of life is not destroyed, but perhaps, using another value scheme, continues, at least on an energetic level, to behave and to occur.

If Death is not oblivion, but just the absence of certain power and activity, then Death assumes a new place in our horizon. It's the time of evaluating the achievements of the person. What has he or she achieved in this world? Is the world any better because of this person? These are all pertinent questions. In my sixty-plus years as a functioning rabbi, again and again I have been confronted by Jews and non-Jews alike: What happens to us after we die? My answer usually is, if you want factual evidence, I can't give you any. I have not met anyone as yet who entered a place where beings exist who, up to that point, had been alive and are now no longer living, perhaps existing.

I, as a Jew, feel if I am to be judged, the measuring rod would be, "Now you are a living being. Go out and take care of the world." It's the words, according to our tradition, spoken by Hashem to the first human when awarding him the task of his existence.

Therefore, at the time of death we are asked by whoever the interrogator may be, "How shall we remember you? What have you accomplished? To whom did you stretch out a helping hand? What fields did you tend, what streams did you purify, which stranger did you befriend, which stranger did you bring into your domicile?" Some of us are ready to give answers, but unfortunately, many are not. Some people have said to me, if I had doubts about going to Heaven after I die, I wouldn't want to live. Some people said it doesn't make any difference what you do or don't do. God loves you. He'll let you into his quarters. Some of us dream about living in Eden someday, the place of luxury and of dainty delight. In some religious quarters, people bent on committing suicide for a higher cause will tell you time and again that the award of their deed is living in the Garden of Eden.

This mythology—for that's what it is—is an ancient rationale for "good living." Why bother living a good life if no one is assured of something greater once your body no longer functions or performs. Its roots, I'm sure, are to be found in the earliest stages of evolution. We know from studies of the evolutionary stages that there was a point when, for safety's sake or for the sake of continued living, leaders arose in the animal packs and helped establish a code of living and procedure. Abide by the code and you are assured of gifts greater than you can imagine or beyond the ken of one's ordinary existence.

We would propose that our tradition is trying to tell us eternal life is impossible. Different stages and forms of life, yes. Eternal life for stage one and its actors is not possible. If you recall in the creation story of Genesis, the Human is told He/She may not eat the fruit of certain trees lest they become "divine," meaning "beings who will live forever." Living forever is not a human possibility. Therefore, one may ask, what happens to us after our bodies cease functioning? During the Middle Ages when this question was discussed from every angle, the consensus seemed to be that a part of us is eternal and lives forever so to speak. But that part no longer has "the human aspect." That part is a state of Being whose energy is invisible, but whose proof of existence is sensed in us almost from birth. Therefore, in our funeral or burial texts, we are told a part of us ascends or separates Itself from us and unites with that which is beyond us. It's as if to say the energy contained in such and such an apparatus doesn't remain there forever. In Its separation, It finds solace and acceptance from other Beings living in the same circumstances.

In our Jewish tradition, we find many statements referring to life after death. The concept of life after death is called *tehiyat hametim*. *Metim* is another word for bodies; the subject is, therefore, the coming alive again of bodies that no longer function.

Many years ago, a non-Jewish woman asked me, "Why do Jews bury their dead standing up?" I was intrigued by the question. I decided to go to Augusta and consult the collection dealing with Jewish and other spiritual behavior. The author of one book said, "Jews believe when the Messiah arrives, they will be transported to the Mount of Olives in Jerusalem." He continues: "Jews being a very practical people, in order to save time, bury their dead standing." Of course, as a Jew with many centuries of Jewish life behind me, I was appalled. I had never heard of such a ritual. In fact, there's a great discussion in the Talmud whether you can bury your dead in grottos or in any other way except in the ground.

I continued my search and came to the conclusion the author was attempting to gather together Jewish folklore and he didn't necessarily interview Jews, but listened to the common fare. If the truth be told, there is a mystical notion of *gilgul*, which means rolling, or turning over, or mobility of souls. It's called *gilgul neshamot*. The travelogue of the *neshama*—breath of God—*Soul*—is quite simple. It's not intricate. It becomes intricate when you believe that everything you do is recorded in some great record book and there comes a time of judgment for you for what you have done or not done.

Throughout our long history, especially on the European continent, we Jews faced an ideology that was completely foreign to us—namely, let the functioning idea in your life be, "Thy will be done in Earth as in Heaven." Once you accept this notion, then you can't fight back. You can't say to God, as Abraham did, "Is it possible that the Judge of the Universe doesn't act justly?" We Jews have always said to Hashem, "Wait a moment. Not so quick. We're dependent on you. Why are you silent?"

Many times, we've been answered. I know personally I have. In moments of great despair facing possible defeat, I have turned to the wall and in a crying voice said, "Don't do this to me! I am devoted to You. I believe in You, and if things are not the way they should be, I know I may be wearing blinders. And all I ask of You, Hashem, is to help me remove the blinders and get back on the road that will lead me to You."

This is my faith. And I live by it. It's been with me ever since childhood. I haven't lived the perfect life. I've had frightful moments. But somehow I may find myself saying what gain will there be if my being, my very existence, is followed by *shachat*, the nether world. I feel—at least in my case and I'm sure I speak for many others—we're constantly standing at the brink of shachat; and when we cry out, the bridge that helps us go over the shachat is there for our use.

I recently heard an address by Rabbi Boteach. He said, I have told my non-Jewish friends the difference between us and them is the fact that we don't live by "Thy will be done," but rather by "What can I do?"

Ours is a mitzvah mentality. A mitzvah is an imperative that I somehow feel called upon to perform. It's a mitzvah when I am walking from one side of the street to the other and I see someone struggling to get across the street and I try to help that person. Now that seems simple and obvious, but most people don't act that way. "You shouldn't try to beat the traffic. You should have waited on the other side of the street. Too bad that your pace is too slow. Stay home where you belong. You're too old to be part of daily street walking." The mitzvah mentality would say to me, "Hold on. It's your duty. It's your moment to help this person across the street. Consider the possibility that for some reason or another, you are there and so is the person about whom we're worried, and perhaps it's your specific task to help them across the street."

There are many more examples of possible mitzvah opportunities. If we had a world in which the mitzvah mentality reigned supreme, then terror wouldn't have the upper hand.

The very terrorists would say, "The God I believe in doesn't want me to engage in Holy Wars of Destruction, but rather in Holy Programs of Construction." Think for a moment of the possibilities of mitzvah living. Manufacturers would be very careful and made sure that nothing creeps into their products that is detrimental to human welfare. We wouldn't worry about contaminated eggs, contaminated beef, contaminated drugs. The manufacturer, having a mitzvah outlook, would check, double check, and triple check, making sure the end product is worthy of human consumption.

According to Jewish tradition, we Jews have 613 commandments by which we live. There's a new theory afloat that all the commandments are spelled out in the book of Genesis, the first book of the Bible. The famous Bible commentator, Nachmanidis, said the 613 mitzvot can be found in the ten commandments of Sinai fame. Search in any way you please, the concept of mitzvah is established. The number of mitzvot is open to debate.

Recently, I met with a group of young adults, and we were using the term mitzvah freely. This is a mitzvah, that is a mitzvah, etc., etc. We arrived at a conclusion. A mitzvah by its nature is some act that helps overcome a gap, a break, in the various vessels needed for a full life. Having a home or some structure over your head providing you with shelter is part of the mitzvah vocabulary. We as Jews said quite early on every human is entitled to warmth, to shelter, to a welcoming atmosphere. We said every human is entitled to success in his or her finding a partner that helps him or her to fully love someone in this world.

"You should love your neighbor as yourself" is an extraordinary mitzvah. It implies that you yourself are worthy of love, especially a love that comes from you directed to yourself. Many students of human behavior have wondered about self-love. Some called it the narcissistic tendency that everything in this world has to do with me. And I have no space in myself for others. Yet, many commentators came to other conclusions. They said how can I possibly love another if I despise myself, if I denigrate myself, if I scold myself, if I deny myself any credit for what I've done and achieved.

As a rabbi, there are times when I am called to officiate at a funeral service. I am expected to deliver a eulogy which praises the deceased. Throughout my 67 years of rabbinic service, I have always interviewed the family of the deceased. I seek a picture, a story that can help me show the positive and contributive side of his or her life. It never fails. Every person at some point in his or her life performed a memorable act. Earlier I spoke of the author of the *Tanya*. Remember I said his greatest teaching was the inherent *tov* or good within each person. We spend a lifetime trying to find out what it is or how it expresses itself. It's there, waiting to be discovered, waiting for the moment when the good within ourselves becomes the telling act of our life.

The debate wondering about the viability of DNA is not our debate. We Jews have always believed in continuous creation, continuous revelation. Hashem is in a state of becoming and so are we. Working with this assumption, we are never lacking for answers or approaches to life's problems.

We Jews have always said there is something undiscovered within us. No one can ever boast of being a complete or fulfilled human being. There lie within us so many secrets which our soul, our spirit, acquired over the generations. Many of these secrets, we feel, are the very essence of what is needed in order to make the world whole or complete, as if to say, we don't need miraculous breakthroughs for change to occur. What we do need is faith in ourselves and faith in that which lies hidden within ourselves. That's part of the partnership we have with the Creator.

A story is told of a man who was the supervisor or manager over an estate. He had his assignments and the owner expected him to live by a planned schedule. In this month or this week, this and that will be done; in another week, another assignment is to be carried out. Once the caretaker became lax. The fruits of the season were of lesser value than of the previous year. The beauty of the land was dulled because the caretaker didn't consult his calendar or his program to fulfill his daily tasks. The owner of the land was disturbed. He called his caretaker and asked for answers. Why are we lacking in color this year? Why is our fruit secondary in comparison to others? What has been missed? How many hours a day have you been spending at the fields? How many times have you read the written instructions? The caretaker hemmed and hawed. It was obvious he had been lax. The owner said to him, thanks to your lack of effort, our status has gone down. The health of our land is impaired. The purpose of our mission is compromised. What can we do to rectify it? The caretaker said I promise I will pay closer attention. I promise I will live up to expectations. I promise I will consult the daily directions. The owner said that's bandaid work. I am looking for creative answers. Can you provide them? The caretaker said, no, my lord.

The owner found himself in a dilemma. Should he fire his caretaker of many years? Or should he say to him and to himself, the dormant is still waiting for your call. He chose the latter. They continued their life tasks; and though they may have lost something along the way, they gained a bond which spoke of trust of each other.

That's the way it is in life. There's always something waiting to be discovered. There's always something waiting to be addressed. Professor Mordecai Kaplan once said in class that when a scientist discovers an answer to a problem in his laboratory, he has uncovered what has been lying dormant. When he discovers it, he is doing God's work, continuing his role as God's appointee on earth.

It's been said the answers to the current economic crisis can be found in the discards of society. Think for a moment. People who travel from one corner of the country to another, poking their noses into heaps of discarded items and then buying them for an acceptable price and selling them for unsuspected millions, are really the new pioneers.

All great inventions have a history. The same is true with all that life calls for. Here in Maine, for instance, we have many people who are deeply involved in the question of energy. The windmills are sources of energy. The many places where water is moving it becomes a source of energy. Some people have created the fuel needed for our mechanized instruments from waste, from woodchips, and from other things that most of us wouldn't even consider in our households. It shouldn't surprise us. The early inventions of energy-driven motors and of batteries took place in Maine. The early adventures which led to air flight took place in Maine. We can go on and on. The lesson is simple. One never knows what lies hidden in the corner of one's home.

I have a family acquaintance who was unemployed for many years. He kept himself busy by scrounging in discarded heaps, refurbishing them, and selling them on e-bay. In fact, he once bought something for $30.00 and by the time he was through with it, he sold it on e-bay for $800.00.

One never knows what lies in abeyance, waiting to be discovered, waiting for the moment when it can announce its presence. Carl Jung once said the inner life is the true life. The outer life is the projected life.

We can never escape the hidden. It finds its way to the surface. Sometimes it comes in a friendly manner, and sometimes it is angered by the many rejections it received.

The story is told of two brothers who lived on opposite sides of a mountain. One was poor, the other was forever finding means of bringing hidden stores to the surface. One day, a famine hit that part of the world. The poor brother said it's just a little more of the same. The wealthier brother said I still have something left. Perhaps I should share it with my brother. He whispered to his wife, "That's my destiny. I feel I've been placed on this earth to take care of my younger brother."

The next morning, he prepared himself for the long journey over to the other side of the mountain. He arose before sunrise, saddled his horse, and went, hoping to reach his brother by the middle of the night. Wherever he stopped, people wanted to know who he was and where he came from and wondered why a man who, in appearance was quite wealthy, would be in search of someone who was not. After all, his appearance placed him in the category of public acclaim. He was wealthy and most likely powerful, in control of a good part of God's earth. Why, therefore, would he spend his days and nights traveling the long distance to meet his impoverished brother?

These questions were asked very forcefully by some. He felt the bond of brotherly love should never be open to question. It is part of nature itself.

He crossed many hills and valleys and finally arrived in his younger brother's village. Upon entering the village, he saw a group of children playing at the village gates. He asked one of them, "Do you know my brother, Chayim?" "Oh, of course we do. Chayim is a nice man. We're always invited to come into his home, and we can always rest assured that wherever we go and we mention Chayim's name, we will be welcomed with open arms."

Big Brother arrived at Little Brother's house. They spoke to each other. They exchanged news and told the wonders of their parents. Big Brother had his store of tales, Little Brother had his own. One day, Big Brother said to himself, I am satisfied Little Brother is doing all he can so that we can be forever bonded. He asked his little brother, are you hungry? Oh, no. God provides. Are you worried about tomorrow? Oh, no. God provides.

Big Brother assured Little Brother a provider will always be available. How do you provide for yourself? Little Brother answered. Frequently, a neighbor will tell me the sorrows of the day. But then sometimes he will share with me the day's joys. I know when he speaks of joy, he wonders why and how did it happen. I feel the same about my life. Every so often, a bit of joy penetrates my environment.

Our great Jewish teachers have always taught us that as long as we are in partnership with God, we will never want for anything. A commentator said its meaning is obvious. God sees us as partners in the caring for the world. Furthermore, God knows that within us reside the answers to all of the puzzles of daily existence. God opens our eyes, our hearts, and our minds. God knows who'll eventually be the partner of our lives. God attempts through his messengers to bring us to the destined providers who will help us in facing our existence.

We Jews never say I'll just sit back and God will take over. We do sometimes challenge God and say, "You expect allegiance from us and yet when we call on You, You seem so silent. Is it possible? What are we missing?"

Why do we feel that God has forgotten us or abandoned us or turned aside from us? Why can't we say the answers are within us and bring ourselves to a point of inner examination which will lead us to the corner that we are expected to turn?

Many years ago, someone called me and said, "Rabbi, I understand you like to hear people's dreams and help them figure it out. I need your help." The person came to my office and told me the following story: "Over and over again, I fall asleep with a dream in my mind's eye. In this dream, I always see a head coming out from a corner. And when I follow it, it disappears. My simple mind tells me a dream image of this sort points to a guide or a messenger ready to lead us to an answer for whatever may be troubling us. Why can't I find out who the guide or leader might be?"

We sat, we talked. Finally I asked, "If you had pencil and paper, could you draw me the face of this dream figure?" The counselee said, "Yes."

I handed him a pencil and paper and urged him to draw. He did. The figure that emerged in part looked like him and in part looked like another. I therefore assumed the dream is an authentic dream and so is the message. The message is you have something inside you that is the key to the doors you want opened. It seems to come and go. Perhaps it feels that you are not ready to assume all the consequences for this dream imagery.

We parted, promising to meet after the counselee has made ten days of notes in his daily journal. Why ten? A dream is always a sacred document. It comes from something greater than our immediate ego. It has its own set of ten commandments and urges you to pay heed. Regard these commandments as seriously as you regard the commandments from the Book of Exodus.

In this case I suggested the ten commandments might be as follows: 1) The God spirit awaits you. 2) Don't compromise it by looking for answers to your dilemmas in places other than your inner self. 3) Not everything is of God; therefore, be careful in your labeling. 4) You must find for yourself some sacred time to fathom the meaning of yourself and the meaning of God. 5) Be always mindful of your roots. Consider yourself a tree planted in the verdant garden, drawing nourishment from its roots and the ground in which it is located. You will especially find this to be true in your later years when the primal source from which you stem is ready to nourish you again. 6) Weigh your words and seek constantly opportunities for honest dealings. 7) Don't steal. 8) Don't kill. 9) Don't break families apart, and 10) Don't be envious.

If you can live by this code knowing that your choices come from yourself, not because someone told you so, but rather your own soul told you so, you'll find life to be a great moment of existence.

Remember we consider this document, or better, this piece of work, to be a dialogue between ourselves and our *inner self*. The dream tells us what the *inner self* is doing and thinking. The dream tells us how far we are ready to go in putting our own mark on life.

VI

Let's continue with the notion of "the dream is our teacher and guide." We are assuming there lies within us—tucked away under layers and layers of lifetime experiences—the original message of our lives. In psychological terms, it is known as the *psyche*. In the dream we just discussed, the psyche is that figure beckoning us from the other side. We found that figure when we descended into our inner cellar. That figure is standing at an intersection where two aisles converge. I was free to go either to the left or to the right. The figure seemed to be on the right. It had a faint smile on its face, and I sensed an energy coming from this figure drawing me to it. I continued descending the cellar steps, ready to follow the figure. The dream ended.

Over the years, I've had such dreams and continue to feel the presence of that figure. It is psyche personified. It is the message intended for me, and I have sought and wondered what it is trying to convey.

I feel the same thing can be said about human life. Most of us are unaware of any inner messages. We're deeply attuned to the world around us and ignore the world or the messages within us.

Over the centuries, we Jews have been at the forefront of many new insights and adventures. We boast of the many Nobel-prize winners among us. Hundreds of tomes have been written about Jewish learning and yearning. Some call us "the people of the book." They miss the essence of the Jewish message which is: *there is lying within you, buried under the debris of daily existence, a guiding light that tries to bring you to the point where you can become the contributor to the healing of the world.* If you recall the passage in Genesis when the first human is told, "Now you are a living being, go out and take care of the world." No attachments, no modifiers are included in that statement. You and all your human descendants are caretakers of the world, not Jewish humans, not purple humans, just humans.

It's an extremely democratic notion. When the prophet Samuel is confronted by a delegation and asked for a ruler or a king comparable to those groups or nations that surrounded the Israelites, he warned them: "Royalty breeds class." Royalty demands absolute loyalty and service. Royalty sees itself standing in the place of God. One pays a heavy price for such political arrangements. He was true to his word. The first king, Saul, suffered. The next king, David, suffered; and the next king, Solomon, the greatest of the kings, the one with the most extensive empire, suffered terribly.

Our tradition has taught us that all who accept the Jewish way of life are members of a holy community. We are all *kohanim*. For lack of a better word, priests, or better still, individuals who are directly involved with God and God's enterprises. We are a *goy kadosh*, a holy nation, a group of people who are on a separate track unlike everyone else, a group of people who have a vision that places the human on the road leading to true human fulfillment.

Throughout the centuries (remember the beginnings of what we call Jewish life was approximately 2000-1800 before the common era), many attempts were undertaken to date our origins. The Bible as we read it attempts to present a chronology. Many scholars have attempted over the centuries to present a firm chronology. Our sages of the Talmud taught there is no chronology in our Bible. *In other words, in many cases it's a collection of incidents, in which the author or authors of the Bible sensed the dynamic of what is Jewish life.*

When we attempt to analyze the Scripture text and we seek and search for what we consider to be the proving points for which the Torah or the Tanach stands when defining the concept of a kingdom of *kohanim* and a holy nation, we sense the inner debate of the author(s) of the sacred text.

The concept of a nation of kohanim, or better still, a holy nation, is unique. For someone to say that it's the most natural thing for humans to strive for this level of holiness or distinctiveness is attributing powers to humans that are usually reserved for divine figures. We Jews have never said the human is incapable of ascending or coming close to the concept of *Divine*. Our rabbis taught us that we have such capacity. We attribute to God a sense of compassion, of caring. So we should be. We expect God to be just. So we should be. In fact, the rabbis say, by nature we who see ourselves as part of the Jewish experience are compassionate and descendants of compassionate people. Again and again we are urged to welcome the strangers among us, to recall the many servitudes that we've experienced throughout history, to point out to ourselves at large and to the world at large that we don't indulge in vengeance, in suicide bombings, in teaching the most horrendous acts as being the passport to heaven's gates.

Recently Rabbi Arthur Green wrote a book entitled, *Radical Judaism*. Rabbi Green asserts Judaism's message was always a universal message, one that said that nothing stands in the way of reaching the highest levels of existence. The highest level is the universal level. When I stretch out my hand and hold on to another and he or she does the same, the chain of caring and compassion grows. We know there is hope.

Forty multi-billionaires recently undertook a pledge. Half of their assets will be devoted to bringing the less fortunate scattered throughout the world to a better existence than they have ever known. Their funds are now being used in Africa, in Asia, in Europe, South America, and wherever the need may arise. No one asked them to do this.

The inner voice speaks: "We are all a kingdom of *kohanim* and a sacred nation resides in us, too." It's a radical idea.

Until recently, the common expression was, *the privileged have the beck and call, the right to demand special consideration.* They assert that *their* power sustains the universe; therefore, they should not be taxed and trusted forever. They will take care of the less fortunate. It hasn't turned out to be that way. The privileged only gain more power. Recently a bureau in the Department of Agriculture responsible for the blockade of Iran has issued over 400,000 permits to assist Iran. In so doing, they have shown that their code is not our code.

Jewish tradition teaches us, "Don't rely on princes. Their promises are seldom kept." Each one of us is a world on its own, connected to the larger world. Each one of us has the power of fulfillment. The Hebrew word for fulfillment is *yeshuah*. It's not the privileged few who are the possessors of fulfillment. Every time we perform a mitzvah—a positive commandment of a repairing and healing nature—we are bringing the ultimate yeshuah closer to fruition. Our tradition taught mitzvah (positive commandment) goreret stimulates yet a further mitzvah act. Whenever we perform a mitzvah, we hasten the coming of the person who best represents a life of total mitzvah—the *Mashiach*.

Accepting this notion, we can understand in a clearer way the text that says, "Now you are a living being. Take care of the world." That first being signified the ultimate being that God had in mind. Every one of us is a reflection of that being. We are all descendants of that being, and that first being's potential lies within us. We Jews never said the human is a fallen being. We said that the human sometimes slips and trips and takes the wrong road, but always has open for him or her the road that can bring him or her back to the primal perfection, the *living being*.

Accepting this concept, nothing stands in the way. The possibility of a fulfilled life based on the goodness of each other, faith in each other, hope for each other, is a reality.

VII

How do we know if we are truly walking on the path to goodness? According to the sages, "Mitzvah goreret mitzvah." One mitzvah brings on another mitzvah. For instance, if I helped an older person to navigate a street corner and helped him or her reach the safety of the other side, he/she will remark, "What a nice person." In making that statement, he/she is performing a mitzvah. He/she is bringing to light my positive creative side. The more positive we feel about each other, the less suspicious we are of each other, and the better will be the mood of all. Currently, pessimism pervades the entire scene. We feel the institutions cannot be trusted; we feel the spokesmen of the institutions are too self-centered; and we feel the need for radical change in our outlook and activities. How many of us are ready and willing to follow in Ghandi's footsteps? How many of us are convinced that a quiet word can move raging mountains?

Some of you who are reading this text might say that I'm naïve. The goodness of which I speak isn't there. The tension I decry is all-pervasive. How many of us are truly committed to live a life of absolute truth? How many of us are saying what they don't know won't hurt them—giving ourselves excuses for trespassing into another person's domain. The statistics we read in the newspaper disturb us. A day doesn't pass without headlines on the front page describing and decrying those who are hell-bent on cutting corners and avoiding the truth.

Many have been asking: Why are we having so many natural catastrophes? The heavy snowfall, the all-pervasive black ice on our sidewalks. Daily, documents proving that "the mighty have fallen" come to light. Recently we were told of a former Swiss banker who provided secret data to the press. The data proved that many important people were running to Switzerland so they could avoid their tax obligations.

The prophets tell us time and again things will change. God's anger will subside. The lonely and the abandoned will be welcome home again. We all know the many stories of the prodigal sons, whether they appeared in the New Testament or in the Midrashic literature. Each corpus had its story of the son who lacked nothing, left home hoping to fend for himself, and discovered there is an end to his resources; and if he is to continue with life, he must reestablish his relationship with his parental bosom.

Thomas Wolfe said that we can never go home again. Both, the New Testament and the Midrash say, "God awaits you. You can go home again." What does going home mean? Does it mean that all of our childhood needs will be met again? Or does it mean the string, the name, or whatever identifies you is never broken or destroyed? Perhaps the Papa that I knew in my younger years has aged. But the love that he had inside himself is still there. For the tie that is love is never severed. Something inside of ourselves urges us on, hoping the broken circle can be mended.

Throughout the world today, individuals, families, clans are seeking to reconnect. The reconnection takes place successfully when divisions of today relate to those of yester-year, but are not duplicates of the years gone by. We can't come home to Papa or to Mama and say, "Years ago, you promised me such and such." Today, we are in another place. Yet we want the warmth, the taste, and the embrace of the yester-year. Papa or Mama might say to us, "It's always been there, waiting for your claim to it. I've never denied your existence. Nor did I ever deny your connection to me or mine to you. If there was a separation between us, it was something of the outside world that tried to impinge and possibly swallow up whatever distinguishes us. Now that we've both matured, we know each one of us in our own way has been on the quest of our own self and of our own soul." If we're honest, we will say that the essence of the old self and the old soul is still here for the taking.

The search, the quest continues on in life. It never ends. Until our dying day, we are seeking that inner message which we received in the beginnings of our existence. The inner message tells us who we really are. If you recall, I shared a dream with you. "The spirit posed at a corner of the room beckoning, signaling, in fact calling that we follow it." I know in my own life that spirit has always been near me. At different moments in my life, it tried to prevent me from going in one direction or another. I resisted and had to pay a price for the foolish gesture on my part. The inner spirit is programmed to be our guide. The inner spirit is telling us: Don't listen to what the world is saying. Listen and search for the words that I am trying to bring you.

For many years, I have suffered from moments of instant sleep. Most times when it happens, I am on the dream level. While I am sleeping, oblivious to the world, I will dream. I'll have another story which I hope is part of the inner guide's map. As I am dictating, I remember moments when I was dictating and suddenly, I lost it and I was in a deep sleep.

The other day, I was invited to lunch. My host was a committed Quaker. I suggested we say grace the Quaker way. We joined hands, closed our eyes, and remained silent for approximately two to three minutes. When I opened my eyes, I knew I was praying for something that was troubling me deeply. I felt I had hurt someone and I had to make amends. We discussed at length the world and how the inner silence can be the guide to separate us from the tumult and the turmoil that is current in day-to-day life. We shared some common notions. We talked about the early days of the Quaker tradition; and we realized that on the mystical level, we are both One. The world my friend seeks is similar to mine, a place that fulfills the prophet's saying, "Not by might nor by power, sayeth the Lord."

Too many in our world are convinced the path to victory lies in the domain and the hands of the spoilers. The louder the gun, the more destructive the weapon, the deeper the chicanery, the use of fear and falsehoods to win points—all this is digging the pit into which we may fall.

Nature calls us. She says, "How many more drastic incidents do you require before the inner change takes place?" The earthquakes, the tsunamis, the rains, the storms, the floods, the fires stare us in the face. Yet, our leaders act as if all is well with the world if only we would remain the same. Our leaders seem to feel change is the great catastrophe rather than to say the mistakes of the past have dug the pits of the present.

We wonder what more must be done to us before we can awaken to the world around us. How many more scandals? How many more failures? How many more unemployed? How many more fears of indebtedness must we suffer?

Every single state in the union is crying, wondering where to find the next dollar. The whistle-blowers who uncover the falsehood of organized living are condemned instead of thanked. Thanks to the whistle-blowers, so many pending catastrophes are uncovered. No one can say we're innocent. Whoever was near the sources of power during the past decade was well aware of the games being played by officials and their underlings.

Falsehood shows itself in the molestation of the young on church premises. It shows itself in the many studies that were lately exposed for their lack of integrity. We find more and more cases of graduate students seeking shortcuts rather than pursuing leads that may strengthen their arguments. We find more and more people pointing fingers at those who see new horizons.

We are more concerned with what may happen three or four generations down the road. It is of greater significance than the hunger, the unemployment, and the poor results in our educational system. If our society seems unstable, if the future is frightening, then solutions rather than false tears must be of primary importance to us. Cry as loud as you might, curse the winds and the shadows, nothing will change. But gird yourself, draw upon the well of faith within yourself. You will find the strength you need, the ideas waiting to be discovered.

Our Jewish sages taught us that everything is in God's hands. Yet, the way you approach what God retains is the key, or better still, the door opener. God implanted in us all that we need to heal ourselves and the universe.

Nothing is hopeless. Our great difficulty lies in our *sense* of helplessness. When we say the world is coming to an end, we've lost our hope. We feel bereft of hope. We feel muted instead of being invigorated by hope.

As you advance in life, as you grow older, as your responsibilities shift from others to yourself, you have to be the captain of your own soul. Consult advisors by the dozen. Run to every spiritual counselor you can find. The one who can help you isn't there. The one who can help you stands off in a corner beckoning, pointing, alluding, saying to you, "You can do it. Here take a test. The test says you can do it. Say a prayer. The prayer responds and says, 'You can do it.'"

Do you remember reading *The Little Engine that Could* to your younger children? Do you remember the voice you read in that book? "I think I can, I think I can." Pull the book off its shelf and hear yourself say, "I think I can. I think I can."

You might say, "I can—what?" Persist in your quest and you will find the answer. You might hear the voice that says, "You've done your bit. Step aside. It's time for someone else." Or the voice might say, "All the experiences of life point to this moment, and, gathered together, you will see a pattern which is the pattern you should pursue."

Let me cite an example. A traveler embarks on a journey. He comes to an obstacle lying across the road's many lanes. He stops, looks around, wonders what's going on. But then suddenly he realizes the obstacle lying in the middle of the road lies there ready to join in the journey of life. It is saying to us, an obstacle is never a hindrance. It's the beginning of a helping moment. The obstacle represents many things: first, the basic material needed to build; second, once it is prepared for building, it shares with you its strength and its beauty. There isn't anything in this world devoid of positive consequence. I sense this feeling deep inside of me: nothing in this world is purposeless.

Among the mystics, one hears and reads various interpretations which link the many parts of the human body to deep insights. The eyes mean this and the nose means that. Every part of the body points to a lesson of the spirit. The mystics tell us what is above is below. What is in heaven is on earth. Every thought has a dark side and a great light it is trying to teach.

In her book *This is a Soul* Marilyn Berger tells the story of Doctor Rick Hodes. Doctor Hodes lived many years among the Ethiopians and gained many insights from this poor community. He tried to arrest the insecurity of the Ethiopian people. A young man, Mesfin Yoseph, came to his home. He invited him in and began to bring him back to normal health. He suffered from a terrible infection that affected his heart. Most of his life he was a great walker, able to walk four hours a day to and from school. But then he contracted the disease and it seemed that his very existence was compromised. The tribal doctors tried to help him and failed. At the age of fourteen, he felt he was becoming a burden to his family. He met Doctor Hodes. Thanks to his efforts, Mesfin was restored to health.

Rick Hodes adopted Mesfin. He considered him an extension of himself. This act of kindness was prompted by Doctor Rick's attachment to the Jewish notion of compassion. In Hebrew it is *Rahamin*. He practiced Rahamin wherever he went.

Our sages taught all God asks of us humans is that our hearts be attuned to him. The heart is the seat of the emotions, and if our emotions are guided by the principle of Rahamin, then the healing the world constantly needs will be forthcoming.

There has grown within me a deep feeling that our world and ourselves is in need of compassion. We've experienced in recent years a deep cleavage between us. Those who have learned how to play the financial games of our time are growing wealthier by the minute. We, the rest, are sinking into a dark and deep mire which seems to be without exits. Once we're in that mire, we're stuck. For the mire places us in debt to the haves. They, in turn, have separated themselves from the rest of the human scene.

Compassion is the key that can open the door where we seem to have been forced by circumstances.

What does it mean to be compassionate? What makes us compassionate? I venture the word itself answers the question: come with passion (feeling). It is part of the human equation to want and to be in need of attachment to another. Didn't the Bible tell us it's not good for a human to live by himself? So the dating game goes on. We, the players, are wondering, will we ever find the one who is best suited for us?

Recently, sitting at a lunch table, some of us asked why would anyone take his hard-earned money and just give it away? If it's yours, why not keep it? Why worry about another? Well, if compassion is part of your scheme in life, you'll know why. Your heart will tell you. You can take your surplus and just fiddle it away. Or, if you sense a tie with another, the joy will be in the giving.

We're a young country. In the short period of our existence, we've had many dire moments of economic crisis. Yet there was always someone on the block who sighed and felt the pain of the other and did something about it. We can all tell stories of the Great Depression of 1929, or we can remind ourselves of the generous neighbor who saw to it that no one went hungry.

Selfishness may be part of the human scheme. So is compassion.

Recently, I read an article in a popular magazine. The author of the article said the way out of the current crisis is through the door of compassion. In compassion's realm, sharing plays a primary role.

Every day I read in the newspaper another compassion story. Whenever I read one, I feel as if a sacred service has been committed. In my way of thinking, God wants us to be the caretakers and healers of the world. In Hebrew we call it *tikkun olam*. The world is in constant need of repair. If we are Bible readers, we are well aware of the first assignment God gave to the first human. "Go to it. Take care of the world." At times we humans have responded. More often than not, we were busy pursuing our own agenda which had very little to do with another human being. We no longer can afford that luxury. The world is connected whether we like it or not. What with the internet, computers, and other arms of the media poised and ready to bring forth change. I leave you to your choices. Do what we were assigned to do and be healers although we are constantly tempted to act otherwise.

The art of healing has been given to all of us. In fact, there is a tradition that says when you are standing at the bedside of an ill person and recite a prayer for his or her welfare, you automatically take one thirty-second of the person's illness and replace it with the healing quality of the prayerful words. As if to say each one of us has been given the gift of being a mender and a healer and a caretaker in this world.

The Hebrew word for a healing is *refuah*. When we want to wish each other healing we say, "May God grant you a *refuah shlaymah*—a complete healing." As if to say I have taken it upon myself the mitzvah (positive commandment) of being a messenger bearing the gift of healing.

Many of us shun such tasks or assignments. We find it difficult to believe that we have been blessed with such powers. Many would accuse us of being egotistical in our saying "my prayers or good wishes will do you in good stead." My life has taught me otherwise. I can cite many incidents where from someplace inside of me, the right words were uttered and healing took place. I recall once standing at the sacred wall in Jerusalem and praying for an individual. Unbeknownst to me at that very moment, he was released from the hospital and was blessed with a complete recovery, surviving that moment for another ten years.

I have accepted for myself the role of the intermediary. I feel it's not of my choosing, but it is an assignment I was given prior to my birth. I am continuing an old family tradition. My father and his ancestors were healers of one sort or another. I have in me a mystical strain that always tells me: "No matter what you may be experiencing, there is something beyond waiting for you to discover." Many times when that thought crosses my mind, I will feel helpless. Yet, something happens. I take some deep breaths and go into a meditative state. The anxiety of the moment is transformed into the awesomeness of the outcome.

When we speak of healing, we are considering existence on more than one level. Of course it is addressing the physical shortcoming of the moment; but more than that, it is an attempt to reach the deepest level that may be the instigator of the current moment when healing is called for. In our prayers, many times we ask for *chiluts atsamot*. It is the invigoration of one's bones—or better still, the rejuvenation of one's body. In fact, in some prayers, the phrase is used when we are thinking of individuals who for some reason or another have fallen apart. Many times it seems to me and to others that the period of history in which we find ourselves is one of *chiluts atsamot*. The political body needs repair, our nerve needs strengthening, our hope for the future has to be recovered; and one can hear the voice resounding throughout our places of residence and worship. Please God, restore us so that we may be whole again.

Can we in our time believe that chiluts atsamot will be achieved? Should we throw up our hands in despair and point our fingers at each other; or is this period calling for a moment when the healing can come about if all of us are involved in it? If only we could put aside our pessimism and despair and replace it with the belief and the hope that chiluts atsamot is possible.

Mystics like myself always say the impossible is possible. We draw on powers and sources of strength in ourselves, which in turn are connected to something higher than ourselves. I remember a visit four years ago to the Rhine Valley in Germany. It was a deep experience for me, for I knew from my search that our family name (Skui or Skuja) referred to a forest. I felt the forest was most likely the Black Forest or, in German, *Schwarzwald*. My travel companion was the co-author of my book, *Give Me Two Minutes of Your Time*, Dr. David Trobisch. Recently we spoke about the trip and he reminded me when we were travelling through the Black Forest, he tried to engage me in conversation. My mouth was moving, but not in response to what he was saying. It was as if I were conversing with someone or some power in the forest. Both of us felt this was a profound mystical moment for me. I'm not surprised, because my father's family had come to Latvia after many, many centuries of residence in the Rhine Valley.

Those of us who are mystically inclined wonder about life and death. We seem to feel that life never ends. What we call life is a collection of stages, each with its own experience. I deeply believe in this statement. I am slowly approaching the last decade of a century of life. On April 17, I celebrated my 87th birthday. This year, for the first time in 87 years, the lunar and the solar calendar coincided. My birthday was the day before the first Passover Seder, exactly as it was at the time of my birth. I discussed this fact with Carolyn Casey, one of the most thoughtful astrologers I've ever met. We discussed the constellation of the planets on April 17, 1924, and realized the same constellation occurred on April 17, 2011.

On my 80th birthday she told me that Uranus was in my chart and it meant that the journey of 80 years, which is Uranus's journey, is part of my destiny. It was in my 80th year of life that I began to sense the weakening of my body and the strengthening of my spirit. It's now seven years later; and looking at it in mystical terms, another creation has occurred in this period of my existence. I am now experiencing its sense of Shabbat, which is spiritual wholeness, and I am poised to enter a new realm of existence. I am changing my place of residence and moving to a part of this country that is suffused with mystery, healing, and reinterpretation of life.

All of this falls under the heading of healing. There are many people in this world who for some reason or another believe the power lies in the hands of someone greater than themselves, and it's arrogance on their part to believe that they can affect the healing process. Their motto is, "Thy will be done," as if God's will and our will are separate. My learning and tradition tells me it's all one, that each one of us is a channel for God's healing. Didn't God say to the first human, now you are a living being? Go out and take care of the world? You are a channel. You cannot separate yourself from the process that keeps the world alive and ticking. The Torah told us hunger will never cease from the land; but at the same time, you are the healer. You can repair it.

God has provided us with people, plans, possibilities, projects—all of them for one purpose: to bring healing to the world.

There are times when we seem to be in a state beyond healing. Our pains speak loudly. Our sense of distance grows. Try as we may, we fail to serve as our own or someone else's healer. Many obstacles arise. What stands in the way is not only germs or bacteria, but also attitudes of mind. They can be as toxic as the most virulent invader of our bodies.

Just think for a moment. You are walking down a corridor and suddenly, you feel as if your very breath has left you. You wonder why. The answers evade you, and you say to yourself "what's going on?" If you have presence of mind, you know that you must stop "dead in your tracks." You must regain your sense of wholeness. It's just drifting by. I shared with you a few pages back my remedy: The ten deep breaths. And every time I do it, at breath six, I sense in my mind's eye a different mood and a different view. In fact, there have been moments, after I have reached breath six or seven, I just started to laugh. People wondered what sort of being is this? One moment he's downcast and the next he's laughing. All that is the essence of the mystical moment. In the Talmudic and the Christian literature, you have examples of individuals who feel they are grappling with some dark force and they have come out victorious.

Don't be surprised. You will recall the story of Jacob and the dark angel who tried to defeat him during the dark night. Jacob won; and the angel said to him: "Your name now shall be *Yisrael*, the one who fought with God and with man and was victorious." The power of overcoming the negative feelings with which we are constantly being struck is there. Take hold of it and let it be your weapon. Didn't Jacob say, "With my staff, which was my only weapon, I crossed the Jordan and was able to go home again"?

Since childhood, I have felt that the stories told to me by my father, the stories I picked up in the Midrash, the stories that I picked up from various books I read or movies I saw were as real as life itself. Oftentimes, these stories come to mind. When I need an answer to a pressing problem or when I don't understand that moment in my life, stories are the storehouse for new moments and new ways of doing things.

These stories strike me as the GPS of these days. All you have to do is tell them what you are looking for and the map appears and the voice of the director can be heard.

The same is true with these stories. They seem to have a voice of their own, ready, poised to act as the guides in your life. For instance, when I was twenty-two years old, having completed my studies at Yeshiva University and being enrolled as a student at the Jewish Theological Seminary, it occurred to me that my life was out of balance. I spoke to a friend who was a practicing psychologist, and he suggested to me that I see an extraordinary psychoanalyst, Dr. Eva Rothman. I made an appointment, I went to see her, and I told her my problem. She came to an early diagnosis, and I would see her three times a week over a period of four years. I sensed she was helping me remove layers and layers of peeling, very similar to the layers that you would find on an onion or a piece of garlic. The closer you came to the core, the more odorous the moment seemed to be.

After four years with Dr. Rothman, I was ordained and went into the open field. I still felt unsteady and still consulted various analysts trying to get to the bottom of it all.

From 1951 till 1961, I wandered from place to place, always looking and hoping I'll discover the core. In 1961, I struck gold. I was elected to be Rabbi of Temple Beth El in Portland, Maine. I retired from Beth El in 1992 and became involved in lifelong learning for seniors. I was instrumental in founding the Osher Lifelong Learning Institute (OLLI). There are now many, many branches of OLLI throughout the United States. And I pride myself for having been instrumental in helping create this wonderful institution.

I tell this to you because every step of the way, from 1946 till today, I felt and I continue to feel that there has been a guiding light and voice within me. Oft times, this light and this voice will tell me my reaction to the world around me is not in sync with myself, as if to say, my *self* has a map of its own. This map, according to my belief, has been with me from the moment I became a fetus within my mother's womb. There are many terms used for this map and many legends pertaining to this map. For instance, in rabbinic legendary sources, we are told the soul is privy to all wisdom. Prior to its entry into the womb, an indentation is made under the fetus's nostril hoping thereby to erase all of the pre-natal wisdom. Isaac Bashevis Singer popularized this legend in many of his stories.

All legends, no matter the source of their origin, are based on someone's insight. The same is true for this legend. The Torah tells us that prior to human creation, God had infused in the nostrils of the yet to be realized being (the first human or Adam) part of God's self, God's wisdom, or all that is without beginning or end. There must be some explanation for the fact that some humans seem to possess all wisdom (example Albert Einstein, Louis Ginsberg) while others don't. As if to say, some of us have made better use of the journey and fathomed more than others. In fact, Isaac Bashevis Singer tells the story of the human soul that was allowed to enter the fetus before being purified. In other words, the soul went into consciousness with information not possessed by others.

Legends abound. In every realm of human activity, there are legends hoping to help solve the riddles of life. Sometimes they do, sometimes they don't. In fact in certain circles these days, one can hear of people who are channels. Through them, divine wisdom comes from above or some other place, and if you want answers in your life, you turn to them because they possess them.

So many of our contemporaries shun legends, yet run to the movies, turn on the TV, listen to the strangest stories, but will never say these stories are sometimes the very foundation for their own bizarre behavior.

In many ways I feel different from my contemporaries. I live and wallow in the realm of legends and dreams. My experience with the insights of Carl Jung and his followers have led me to inner journeys uniquely my own. For many years I have felt that my birth was not complete. I can point to wakeful moments or dream moments and say they pointed me in a direction that turned me into a channel. As if answers to life and whatever else may concern me at the moment were not to be found in ordinary ways, but in deep inner thoughts.

I especially call to mind a journey. I dreamt that in an old basement I had discovered a discarded child. I embraced it; and years later, I felt I discovered the discarded child in a cave and I brought it forth. Finally I found myself on a voyage on the raven's back, which brought me to a celestial palace; and I heard the raven turned human say to me, "You are not only of the human world, but you have roots in this upper world. At times you go to the human, always bringing it a message, trying to steer it back to the inner maps that it possesses."

I've known for many years that we humans live on many planes. Oftentimes when we seem at odds with others, it's not our fault. We have found ourselves and the other has found itself. Sometimes we meet, sometimes we don't. To me, the spiritual quest seems to be each one of us attempting to find our own inner core—being able to point to something and say, "This is who I am, though it may take me in directions different from the community in which I live."

I apply these criteria to all aspects of life. "To thine own self be true" is a maxim. As a Jew, I believe the essence of our Jewish message is: "You have within yourself a truth that is your own." As I said above, it's part of your assignment. This is how you can become one of the healers of the universe, one of the menders of the tears that exist within our lives. That essential truth is the Jewish journey—finding the truth that is yours, recapturing the part of eternity taken from you prior to birth.

VIII

We Jews have always believed we are an eternal people. Abraham, the first Jew, was assured by God that his descendants will never perish from the earth. To me it means there may be casualties in various moments of history; but the essence of our existence is here to stay. What is that essence? Finding your true self, knowing your place as a healer of the universe, and being forever hopeful and positive in your life's outlook. In other words, we Jews never will admit that any path on which we happen to be is the final path. We are the eternal wanderers forever seeking that great place. In Jewish folklore, the great place was sometimes called *Sambatyon*. It was a mythical place beyond all mountains, the place where the *Mashiach* (Messiah) will be revealed.

The legend of Mashiach has many levels to it. First, prior to his arrival, Elijah, the ancient prophet, will announce his coming. Elijah himself is a modest being. He isn't dressed in a knight's armor or in any royal garb. In some versions of the story, he is sitting on a street corner dressed in shabby clothes, winding and unwinding the bandage on his foot. Elijah is always welcome at the *bris* (the eighth day after birth when male children are circumcised). At the service that separates the *Shabbat* from the rest of the week (*havdalah*), we sing about Elijah's coming. At the *Passover Seder*, we open the door to welcome Elijah. He is a mythic figure; yet, he resounds with deep concerns and implementations.

Elijah was never perceived as a great military hero, a conqueror, one who defeated the masses. If anything, his humility is his ultimate strength. Elijah, in the tales of the Bible, lives in hiding for some time, as if to say he's incapable of confronting a military figure.

This shouldn't surprise us, for the motto is, "Not by might, but by My spirit," says God. In Judaism, it was never felt that military power is a sign of anything. Military power is sheer boasting that will, in time, melt away. The simple one, the courageous one, the loving one, the compassionate one is God's servant. If you read the Bible stories, the antagonist is always a military figure. The one who saves you is the kind, compassionate one.

I knew quite early in life that the way of the bully was not my way. At times I tried to befriend the bully, but I ended up with pie in my face. The bully is not interested in coming to terms with others. His interest lies in overcoming others, destroying them, and making them cringe and many times beg for mercy. I was attracted from early childhood by soft colors, the pastels, and not by the shadowy colors.

What does this tell me? What is the direction that is mine? How did I enter this life? What was my assignment? I knew quite early that I harbored a voice which whispered constantly to me, "Forgive. Encourage. Embrace."

IX

In my lifetime, the human race has experienced many cataclysmic moments. We've suffered many economic depressions. We've watched tyrants ascend the thrones of power and insist they brought stability to society. The fact that they used horrendous henchmen to keep this population in line and in tow was ignored by most people. How many times did we hear during the twelve years of Hitler's power that he is to be honored for the autobahn, the trains that ran on time, the discipline and order that was the mark of the Nazi?

Hitler was right when he said no one will raise a voice when I embark on my great program of making the world *judenrein*, devoid of Jewish populations. Many read his infamous *Mein Kampf* and the more infamous *Protocols of the Elders of Zion*. Some smiled, some shrugged their shoulders, and some said that's what the world needs. Strong, strong, definitive leaders. We know the price we paid in honoring people like Hitler.

From 1932 up to the present time (2011), strong leaders have appeared on the horizon. At this moment, we are watching the various rebellions of the Middle East. In Egypt, in Tunisia, in Jordan, in Libya, and many other places, people are standing up and saying we can't live any more under the rule of the autocrat. The *Demos* (populace) has to be heard. The least among us is entitled to a hearing.

Will we ever live to see and witness the true democratic society for which we constantly hope and pray? At this present moment it seems as if all who urged the establishment of a democratic, Egyptian society are buying the humbug of stability proposed by Mubarak and his followers, the stability that is a by-product of beatings, torture, and other deprivations stemming from Mubarak's police and secret agents. Some of my friends sat and watched the TV reports. They're worried about Israel and other communities endangered by the turbulent Middle East. I'm afraid the notion of strength is still the guiding notion of many. When will people realize that the greatest strength isn't the by-product of police beatings, but rather the outcome of dialogue, cooperation? *Ahav* is better for the whole world. It is the linking of one another.

Many translators of the Torah say *Ahav* means love. I differ with them. Ahav means linkage. You shall link yourself to another as if that other was you. No autocrat would ever allow this feeling in his society. The linkage of which we speak when we use the term Ahav is an embracing one. It brings many under the shadow of your wings. It says to the distant stranger, "You needn't feel so separate from us that we can't talk to each other." It is the driving force of compassion.

X

Both the charter of the League of Nations and the charter of the United Nations tried to introduce a sense of *Ahav* into the realm of politics. They failed. Stability was a guiding principle. We must have stable governments, we must have stable economies, we must have stable relationships formed with one another. For the sake of stability, we've sacrificed justice, compassion, and the sense of caring for one another. Will we ever learn our lessons, I sometimes wonder. The world hasn't learned its lessons in the eighty-seven years that I've been on this earth. Why should I believe they will in the future?

Every cloud has a silver lining, the poet tells us. There's truth in that saying. In the darkness that is society today, we see little pockets of individuals who have dedicated a good part of their personal fortune to the amelioration of hunger, disease, joblessness. But unfortunately, it's never enough. Headlines may bring good job offers. They don't necessarily resolve human social ills.

Throughout my life, singular questions loomed in my mind: Why? Why this? Why that? I posed that question to my father when he told me, "A good Jew does this or a good Jew does that." I asked, "Why?" His answers were always traditional; in other words, this is the way it's always been and so it shall continue. The origin, of course, is God, the revelation on Mt. Sinai that my parents taught me. Wherever you turn, you find Jews behaving this way.

At the age between five and seven, those answers pacified me; but from seven onward, my *whys* became more widespread. Why do we celebrate Hanukkah? So what if, during an assembly, I join in the singing of Christmas carols and by mistake, or perhaps by choice, I pronounce Jesus' name? Or better still, why do we Jews insist that we as humans are different from non-Jews? Now remember, these are questions being posed by a child at the age between seven and eleven. In those days, I asked other questions. Why about boys and why about girls. Why about brothers and why about cousins. Why about father, why about mother. But the most urgent question for me was simple: Why has God made the kind of world we seem to be in?

Now remember I was seven in 1931. The heat of anti-Semitism was growing in leaps and bounds: Father Coughlin, Colonel Lindbergh, the English Duke of Windsor, the Astor crowd outside of London, and of course the Nazis. Their admirers and followers were turning up the heat and making life miserable and uncomfortable for those of us who called ourselves Jews. It's an error to say that anti-Semitism was only in Germany. It was worldwide. Many, many gates were closed to German-Jewish escapees. The borders of Switzerland were closed; the borders of America were closed. And the borders elsewhere were closed.

During that period of 1931-32, it was the topic of daily conversation; and organizations sprang up like flowers and weeds in defense of Jews, or in acts of denunciation of Jews.

Some saw us as the thirteen old men who gathered in the old Prague Jewish cemetery every Yom Kippur to decide the fate of world populations. That book was first published during the time of the Dreyfus trial; but Hitler and his followers gave it a place of prominence on their bookshelves.

So here I was, a kid at the age of seven, eight, nine, ten years asking, "Why?" No one seemed to have an answer. Only sighs and sorrow. And statistics. Every day stories would appear of other horrendous acts directed against Jews. Some were imprisoned; others were killed. Still others were tortured to death. Most importantly, they were herded into places supervised by believers of the Nazi ideology.

After the war, post 1945, our eyes were opened; and we saw and tasted and experienced the horrors of the Nazi anti-Jewish program.

I'm sorry to say my *Whys* of those days were never answered. We humans were overwhelmed by our specialness. Our scientific achievements, for good and for bad, were the daily headlines—the great machinery of America that outfitted this country so that they could eventually become the victors in Europe. The new insight into many diseases, the deep understanding of cures for broken limbs and broken bones and other casualties of war and torture—all of this was on the daily agenda. Those of us who said that perhaps human behavior triggered some of this evil were scoffed at, dismissed, seen as residents of another planet and another philosophic time.

In my adolescence, my own insecurities fed into the *Why*. I kept on asking myself, what have we, the Jews living outside of Europe, done to rescue and rebuild the lives of Hitler's victims. I remember posing a question at a lecture in 1944. I said, after all, Hitler's *Mein Kampf* was written before 1932. Many people saw the raw pages of *Mein Kampf*. These pages were circulated among Hitler's followers. They in turn shared them with the public. More and more, members of the public said, "Yes, what Hitler said is true. The Jews are our downfall." The German term for the downfall is *Unglück*—our bad fortune.

I was denounced. Someone asked me, "Why didn't you ask God. Where was He all this time?" I said, "God is not a poor parent, one who is always poking His nose into His children's business. God opens our eyes; but if we remain blinded, it is not His fault."

I felt if we're to avoid such occurrences again, then we have to understand the boundaries of personal responsibility.

Since the Second World War, many segments of our population (especially the young adults) have said that our parents' generation has fed us indigestible food, indigestible ideas, indigestible approaches to communal life. We, the younger ones, have taken it upon ourselves to reshape things.

Prayer can move mountains, we've been told. I believe it. My whole life has been a wing and a prayer. Many times I was ready to "cash it in," but a small, still inner voice quietly steered me away from any drastic actions.

The young people of our day who are responsible for the revolts in Tunisia, Egypt, and other countries have a voice of their own. It's not necessarily the institutional voice by which so many of my generation were raised. Institutions have a tendency to further the belief that their answer is the only answer for life. There are Jews who speak that way—Christians and Muslims, too. And who knows what the unknown sects of various parts of the world may be saying. In fact, I seem to feel that each person has their own personal inner voice which lets itself be known. Some would claim this is part of our DNA. Others will say it's a voice that evolves during the first few weeks of life, and its echo is heard throughout our lives. Sometimes we accept it with grace; other times, we stand in opposition to that inner voice.

There have been respectable traditions which have insisted that the personal inner voice is God's greatest antagonist. To be a pious person, they would tell us, you have to squelch the personal inner voice. In the Jewish tradition, there are some who would say it is the *yetzer harah*, the evil inclination, that steers us away from behaving as we should.

I personally don't believe anyone is a captive of the *yetzer harah*. I think all of us can sense and resist the forces that seem to lead us down the path of self-destruction. To completely live a human life, one has to be in tune with other humans, with nature, with one's own inner history. Otherwise, no one would be able to boast that he or she is his or her own person.

The mystics have taught us that our only true voice is our inner voice. They point to the artists of this world, whether they are literary artists, musical artists, or visual artists. It makes no difference. A good and true artist is guided by a voice inside that leads to the point of true self-expression. Many examples can be cited. When the Book of Proverbs said to teach the young person, or better, the adolescent, and to "guide him by his own voice," it was affirming this belief. If you watch children, especially two- and three-year-olds, as their own personal voice is beginning to break through and their insistence that this voice is their true voice, the power of their affirmation makes you stand back and listen carefully. Over the years, I've watched children playing in the preschool playing ground. Some might be considered bullies, but they're not. They are young people with a sense of themselves.

What does it mean to be yourself? How do you know that what you're saying is really yourself speaking and not just the aping of someone else's ideas or voice? What are the criteria for judging these statements? I think, first of all, a person who is convinced of the authenticity of his voice will tell you that in the development of this voice, he felt he reached a point of inner strength and elevation. For example, a young man came to me one day and said, "Rabbi, why should I pay attention to anything you tell me? How do I know that what you're saying is what I really want to say? How do I know the statements you quote from the Torah or other sacred literature were authored by the people to whom they're ascribed?"

My first answer usually is, "Well, you don't know. You just sense it's the right way. You're ready to get up on a soapbox and claim it. That's what the prophets did, whether you speak of Isaiah or Jeremiah or anyone else. Oftimes they would say, 'so speaks Hashem.' They are telling us, "These are not my words; but I've become a mouthpiece, a spokesman, a channel for Hashem." We are told some of these spokesmen resisted the call to speak. Moses did. Jeremiah did. Isaiah did. And who knows how many more? I'm sure in your life and in the lives of many, you just blurted out your statement. You stood up, raised your hand, and shouted out what you had to say. You knew there was a force inside of you stronger than you pushing, urging you to speak; and when you finally did, more often than not, you were soaked through and through, as if to say your very insides cried out."

These are rare moments; and we're not always sure they are authentic moments. But when they are, they will bear results.

XI

Of late I've become convinced sacred moments don't necessarily occur in sacred buildings. I've come to the conclusion that a shaded tree can be as sacred as any cathedral.

Many years ago, my family visited Rome. We entered the great city, we went from one neighborhood to another, and finally, we arrived at Saint Peter's Cathedral. I had heard many stories about the strength of Saint Peter's Cathedral. I entered the building and sat down in one of the corners where the seats faced the pulpit. I closed my eyes and fell asleep. I dreamt a dream. It was very similar to the dream I later had in the Cathedral of Einsiedeln in Switzerland, the cathedral with the Black Madonna.

My analyst, Hermann Strobel, had posed the question: "You've told me about yourself and your late wife, but who are you?" I tried to hem and haw, hoping I was answering him, but to no avail. He advised me to visit the Black Madonna that dwells in the Cathedral of Einsiedeln, Switzerland. The Black Madonna was trying to give me an answer to the question posed by Hermann Strobel. Who am I? And the answer, I believe, lies in the notion that "life is never complete. It is always in a state of becoming." Therefore, we should never find ourselves guilty, but rather say of ourselves: "We are on a journey."

Judaism has always said that. Our system of Jewish living is called *Halacha*. The root of Halacha is the verb *HLCH*. We pronounce it "halacha." Movement, going forward, always seeking, and always knowing if we've erred. The journey never ends. You can always start again.

In every generation, attempts have been made to be part of the world and yet separate from it. Some of the rabbinic commentators based this on an interpretation of what beauty and scholarship are all about—*yaft Elohim l'yefet.* When we say being a complete Jew in your home and an acceptable citizen outside of it, we are granting the viability of the premise that states Jewish survival has been assured by our ability to be the roses rather than the brambles, the beautiful flower rather than the thorns. And we have been successful. Wherever you turn, you will find the fingerprints, the footmarks, the concrete evidence that Jews have been there.

Let's spend a few moments on this statement. No one will deny the existence of astute Jewish physicians from ancient times to the present. It's true there were some within the rabbinic community who distanced themselves from physicians. They claimed physicians were trying to play God. Some rabbis said the physicians were people without faith. They accused the physicians of insisting that the power of healing was in their hands. Many times they'd overstep their boundaries. But then again, the surrounding world insisted that our physicians had access to information and to healing powers of various animate and inanimate objects in our communities.

For example, they felt certain plants were able to act as aphrodisiacs. Other plants contributed to the welfare of other systems prevalent in our bodies. Some people felt the great Jewish physicians were privy to mysterious healing powers and urged these physicians to be retained for the many courts, Christian and Muslim.

There are other examples. Many of our rabbis through the sheer power of observation attested to the latent power of much that grows in the forests of this world. When you read the novella of Medieval times, you'll frequently find references to the prevalent growth of certain plants in your neighborhoods. A wonderful example of such healing knowledge can be found in the series, *Rashi's Daughters*.

The midwives who were semi-physicians in those days would go into the forest at least twice a year and pick the plants they felt were bona fide remedies for all possible illnesses and situations.

The rabbis on the whole felt the physician was God's extension on earth. The physician, through his training and practice, was obviously aware of the nuances found in these medications. Even in our time, one finds people who seem to have a sixth sense and can attest to the power of these products of the earth.

During the middle ages, the Jewish scholar oftentimes had a profession by which he derived the funds necessary for the upkeep of his family. More than that, one finds here and there references to great scholars who were very deeply involved with the secrets of the forest and other foliage. I recall when I was a child a special blessing was recited when a physician came into our house. Many times a royal welcome would be extended to the physician.

The physicians of medieval times were greatly honored by the populace. Nobility and serf stood in awe when the physician came into their abode. In fact, the physician was given the power to decide what words, what prayers, what remedies should be indulged in. The guiding principle was: Whoever saves or rescues a single soul saves the entire world.

Let us return to the Ten Commandments. The second commandment is: "You shall not make for yourself a sculptured image or any likeness of what is in the heavens above, or on the earth below, or in the waters under the earth." Once you give special status to any part of nature, you diminish the totality that is *Hashem* (God). Judaism has tried from the beginning to speak from the aspect of wholeness. All the world is one, all of us humans are related to one another, we're all part of the same creation, we all have the same DNA. Therefore, don't pedal the notion that a part of nature can actually challenge the whole of nature.

The third commandment states: Don't attach the name of *Hashem* (Adonai or God) to inanimate objects. They do not participate in the curative aspects of all that is God.

The fourth commandment should never be dismissed lightly. It is the commandment of Shabbat, of the idea that one has to, every week, stop and take a breather. Otherwise, you'll be consumed by your ambition, by your narrow-sightedness. Every being needs the moment of spiritual rest. No one is immune to the positive and negative aspects of believing and acting in a sacred way.

The fifth commandment deals with family issues. Honor, it says, your parents. Not bow before them, not adore them, not place them on pedestals, but extend to them *kavod* (the honor) of parenthood. When an individual acknowledges the role of his or her parents in their lives, they are also acknowledging the gift of life itself, the acceptance of their own personal DNA.

The sixth commandment urges us not to engage in murder. The rabbinic tradition spent quite a bit of time in analyzing the concept of taking another one's life. They said at times, when you malign someone and cause them great misery, you are taking that person's life. Though there may not be any specific penalty, the misdeed is of profound importance. For instance, if you malign a woman by trying to prove her infidelity, and evidence points to the fact that you, the culprit, invented the story, it is suggested that you suffer the penalty you were ready to impose upon her.

These Ten Commandments were understood throughout the ages to be the pillar for civilized society.

There is a midrash which states that God sent messengers to all existing communities asking them to sign up for the Ten Commandments. Everyone refused except the descendants of Abraham. We, the direct descendants of Abraham and the upholders of the Abrahamic tradition, said we will obey it and pay attention to it.

The next commandment is, "You shall not commit adultery." In our tradition, marriage is more than a private sexual or economic arrangement between two individuals. It is a holy covenant. God's relationship to the Jewish people is seen as a holy covenant. One does not treat such covenants lightly. They are the basis of civilized society.

The eighth commandment is, "You shall not steal." It refers to both property and persons. The snatching and selling into slavery of innocent victims was common in Biblical days. The ninth commandment is, "You shall not bear false witness against your neighbor." When you do, you are absconding with everything that is sacred to your neighbor—his honor, his prestige, his place in society. An example of false witness was the comment made above about infidelity.

Last but not least is the commandment, "You shall not covet." Whoever had the privilege of raising children can attest to the moments when a member of the family would ask for something owned by a nearby friend. The parent would say, "You can't have it." The petitioner would say, "But I want it." The parent replies, "Really? You are living in this house, not in your friend's house." And so the argument increases. Sometimes words are said that are better left unsaid; and therefore, we are left with a great question: When do you give in or when do you insist on your own integrity?

XII

It is our belief that the Ten Commandments, when seen through modern eyes, still retain their novelty. Wherever you turn in this world of ours, one commandment or another is disobeyed. So few people are willing to accept the possibility of the *I* being present within themselves. So few people these days are willing to use as the basis of their activity the essence that is themselves. It seems as if we would rather act from the stance of passion rather than out of personal integrity and personal commitment to the lessons of one's own sense of *I*.

The world is in a state of terrible danger. Throughout the world—east, west, north, or south—there are young people and others waiting for the moment of encounter. Many of them are followers of Ghandi and Martin Luther King's approach of nonviolence. Let's sit down and talk, they seem to say. Those who have been serving in a seat of power feel that power is with them. They will disperse it. They will control it. Others must honor it. The fifth commandment spoke of honoring your parents. Nowhere did it say that honor means to erase your own integrity. In fact, the Biblical tradition suggests that in dealing with our adolescents we try to be their teachers starting at their own place of existence. This revolution is saying that the voice of God resides in everyone, not in the select few. The voice of God is not dependent on your social status or, for that matter, on your achievement on the economic ladder reaching to success.

Another example is the last commandment, "Thou shall not covet." If life is only the satisfaction of my momentary desires and needs, then we are saying those moments of desire and need are my moments and my moments only. Don't ask me to place a burden on my own desires and needs for the sake of others. It is self-centered, and it is saying that none of humankind is connected to each other. This is the earmark of chaos.

Our reading of the Biblical text suggests that prior to the creation of our current world, chaos existed. The text tells us in a succinct way how the chaos was overcome. It came about, we believe, by and through the will of God. It stressed the oneness of this creation. It urged us humans to learn how to live together, one with the other. The first few chapters of Genesis, or as it is known in Hebrew, *B'rayshit*, is a collection of attempts at orderly civilization. It failed because the universe was filled with *hamas*—violence. We have the story of the flood and then of God saying, "I know the humans are not like myself and I must be aware of their way of life. I will never destroy them completely." And the rainbow crossing the sky is His witness or proof.

The Torah seems to suggest: Use nonviolence as your means of coming to terms with each other. The Ten Commandments—every single one of them—points to some form of violence and admonishes us not to indulge in this violence.

The Torah is an extraordinary document. The books that follow Deuteronomy are but examples and exaggerations of all that the Torah taught. It's filled with stories, parables, and what we now call *Midrashim*. These stories, these parables, these *Midrashim* are study aids. Often, stories are needed to illustrate a point. As if to say, nothing is beyond human cognition. For example, in the Book of Joshua, we read the story of the spies who penetrated Jericho. The mistress or guardian of the wall says, we've all watched and we're now convinced no one can stand in the way of your God. And we want to ally ourselves with you, as if to say, "You don't have to fight to win your point. God and God's actions are the winning instrument." We can cite other stories, all with the same purpose—to prove the viability of this universe, the love and care that God extends to it, and the many people floating around in this world who are saying, "I'm ready to join ranks with you."

In Joshua we have stories of individuals asking for acceptance into the Jewish people. We have individuals who, at the time of the Exodus from Egypt, asked to join us. Until this day, most rabbis will testify, that many have come, many have sought to be part of this ancient people.

Strangers wonder from where do Jews come? There are many answers—the answers of the Tanach (the Hebrew Bible), answers from the Midrash (the Rabbinic literature), and answers from the many who joined us during various periods of history. Earlier we had stated the Jews are known as *Ivri*, which for all practical purposes means wanderers or nomads. We were never a settled people. We made attempts at settling. We dreamt of a restored temple in Jerusalem. We dreamt and we dreamt, but we knew inside our own hearts we carried our Jerusalem within us.

What does this mean? First, wherever you may turn, wherever we Jews have lived, we have always managed to integrate ourselves into the world that surrounded us. Sometimes we were merchants. Sometimes we were vintners. And sometimes we were artisans. Many of us were involved in commerce and still others in medicine and in the political process of the land in which we happened to be living.

The point we're trying to make is simple: From where did we originate? The Bible's assumptions are as good as any. The most important thing to remember is: Someone was always knocking on our door seeking entrance. When the Jews left Egypt, they were known as descendants of Abraham, Isaac, and Jacob. They were known as *Ivriyim*. Many legislated against us, trying to stem the tide of those who sought by their own will to become members of the Jewish community.

The major problem faced by us throughout these many centuries of life was the fear others had of us, the fear that gave rise to many negative theories about Jews, Jewish concepts, Jewish living. I lived in Maine for fifty years. Not too long ago I came across an interesting story. Sometime during the 1840's or 1850's, someone had raised the old *Canard* that "Jews take the blood of Christian children to bake Passover matzot." For a while people believed it. Fortunately, there were many who laughed at such idiocies and dismissed them before they could take root. In Europe, especially during the medieval period, far too many people believed this nonsense and legislated against Jews based on fallacious evidence. It can never happen. Jewish law stands in opposition to such thinking. In fact, our tradition teaches us whoever saves a human is rescuing the entire world. Whoever destroys a human is undermining the world's foundations.

We've faced other problems. For some reason or another, some people decided they didn't want to have any relationships with Jews. In the 1930's, the Nazi scourge arose and there were exhibits throughout Germany denouncing the Jew. In fact, one could find on the walls, on the glass windows in front of great department stores, the saying, "The Jews are our misfortune." It took many years and many, many victims before the world said no to this nonsense. When General Eisenhower entered Dachau at the end of World War II, the shock of the scattered bodies, the shock of the odor of decaying flesh affected him; and he insisted that local residents clean up the place, bury the victims, and bring the personnel of the many camps to justice.

Our Jewish tradition is a code for living. It begins with the notion that each and every one of us, male and female alike, have within ourselves a bit of the Creator. We feel the Creator's statement to Adam (the first human), "Now you are a living being. Go out and take care of the world" to be the guiding principle for human existence. When we act in our relationship with humans in a pure way, then our hearts tell us it's springtime all over.

What does *a pure way* mean? Let me share with you my understanding of that term. To be *pure* is synonymous with *KDSH (kedusha)*. My teacher, Abraham Joshua Heschel, once urged us to look at everything through the glass of KDSH. When we say something is KDSH, we are saying that something is in a category of its own. To be labeled KDSH is to envelop something in a different way. It's no longer mundane. It's no longer something like all other things. It has its own value and its own way of relating to other things. If something is KDSH or is behaving in a KDSH way, it is attuned to all that is happening. Whenever a Jewish wedding ceremony is performed, the bride and groom say to each other, "Be thou consecrated (made KDSH) to me as my own." It is spelled out in the codes, in the sayings. It is enunciated by Moses who, in turn, is sharing with us the message of God that he received.

When I say to someone, "You are KDSH and I want to treat you as if you were," I am giving that person an assurance that I won't dismiss him, that I won't mock him, that I will regard him seriously. Whatever statement may be shared by two people who are in a state of KDSH—it's not trivial. It's of great consequence.

KDSH is the root word and it is used in many ways: first as we outlined above, a state of being. A person that is KDSH, is unlike anyone else. Second, a person guided by the KDSH principle will never dismiss anyone or anything. Everything is part of this world. Everything has to be taken seriously. Third, a person who seeks to live by the principle of KDSH will always seek opportunities of mending this ruptured world of ours. That person feels that every act of KDSH (Kedusha) is God driven. That's what God asks of me, namely—never treat anything in life in a dismissive way. Hunger must be addressed. Homelessness must be addressed. Fear and pain must be addressed. That's part of the charge, "Go and take care of the world."

At this point, I would like to share with you the typical day of a person who is living under the banner of KDSH. He arises in the morning and says, "Hurray! I've lived to see another day! I'm looking forward and wondering what is in store for me during this day. If I'm very serious about my KDSH status, then I'm planning a program of mitzvoth—inner-driven activities that are giving me the opportunity to be a caretaker of the Universe." It could be a blessing recited over a piece of bread. It could be something given to a stranger facing one of life's dilemmas. It could be a program of study that will help sharpen my mind so that I could see clearly the caretaker program of which I am an integral part.

There is a Hebrew saying: "Shomer petaim Adonai." God protects the helpless, the wanderers, those who are trying to find their place in life. And we Jews believe it is incumbent on us to imitate the great virtues that we believe God possesses.

The Torah tells us that we must be aware of the stranger, of the weak, of the helpless, of the orphan, of the widow, of everyone who is in one way or another on his or her own without a support system. The Torah in its wisdom recognized as long as humans are on this earth, such cases will be with us. Poverty will never completely disappear; nor will sorrow. We who recognize the truth of this insight are being called to be the great helpers who are deeply involved in *Tikun haolam*, the repair of the world. We deeply believe as our tradition tells us that every day is an act of creation. In our prayers we say it. "God daily creates the Universe." The physicists tell us each day is an act of creation. The astronomers say the same thing. Each day, new planets are discovered and new pockets of energy reveal themselves. We humans have been given the task of staying afoot with all of this information. We cannot dismiss it. If we run away from the world, the ensuing chaos will capture us and we will become its prisoners.

You might ask how do we know what to do? Not everyone is an astrophysicist or a theoretician or a discoverer of latent powers. But we all know in our hearts of hearts that there is a destiny within us seeking to fully play its role in the Universe. Oftentimes we wake up in the morning sensing this is the day for which we prayed. At last it has arrived. At last the map that we have been seeking has been received. At last the journey has become a meaningful enterprise.

When that moment of realization arrives and we see it in the full clarity of our minds, hearts and souls, we feel as if a pure wind or a welcome body of water has passed over us, and we are ready to say "Hallelujah! We need not fear."

In my many years of serving as a rabbi, I have experienced many moments of greatness and many moments of defeat. I've been blessed with the experience of seeing the one who cries out from the depths rise to the top and become the builder for the future. I have met people who were consigned to the heap of the forgotten, the forlorn, and the lost come to see the light and return to civilization. I've witnessed Carl Jung's famous dictum: "Honor a person's myth. Let it be acceptable. Then that person will find his way back to society as a whole."

My life has taught me that *no* is a temporary answer as is *yes*. One has never completely arrived; nor is one ever totally lost. You may be lost in the forest filled with dark highways and byways. You are also privy to the road that will lead you beyond the forest.

What drives us? Faith. I know in the depths of my being that I am living under a protective cloud, the cloud that I seek every evening. In the *Hashkivenu* prayer, we ask that God spread over us His temporary shelter of peace. We also ask that we be the recipients of good advice coming from God. Our faith tells us that the protective cloud of God is always ready and available to us. The problem that we humans have is that we feel God is with us when we get what we want at any given moment. Faith teaches us the gift from God sometimes is not what we ask for. In fact, it may be the very thing we don't want; but somehow, there is a discerning power in this Universe that knows when (a) is good for us and (b) is not.

Life is a journey, a never-ending journey. It starts prenatally and it continues post mortem. Nothing in this Universe is ever wasted. Many times waste turns into the very chemicals we need for survival. If one part of the body is suffering, the rest of the body will realize it. In fact, we can say the same about our psyches. The psyche sometimes speaks to the body that houses it and says, "You've neglected me. You think life is only what you see with your eyes. You forget that there is an old story within you and that has to be catered to as much as the story that you view with your natural eyes." God says to us, "I am here for you. But don't expect me to step in and take over when you need to act naturally. You're the caretaker. Every caretaker knows that if he neglects the garden, it will be destroyed by strange weeds." If we neglect our bodies, latent destroyers hidden in the depths of the colon and elsewhere will find their way into the stream that is life and take it on a misguided journey. Not the journey intended for us, but the journey that brings us to the opposite place.

Since life is a journey, one can never say this or that point is the essence or the core of life. We are the carriers of ancient messages. The reason for our daily activities or the impulse that drive these activities has its roots in our ancient past. In past generations, great attempts were made to discover what influenced us. Some said the stars. Others had other formulas. Whatever the case may be, what we are now is the product of what was.

Jewish tradition has relied heavily on the concept of the past. In our prayers and elsewhere, we speak of the life lived by our ancestors. Every Shabbat morning when we read the Torah portion, we try to peel away the barriers from the words we are reading; and we know in those old, old words, the answers to the puzzles of today will be found.

We have said previously that the word, *Halacha*, commonly translated as *tradition*, is the allusion to the journey on which we are embarked. The root of *Halacha* is *halach*, which means movement. I would like to suggest that Halacha is the euphemistic term used by our ancient teachers to enlighten us and define for us the meaning of the journey. Unlike most orthodox circles, I differ with the accepted notion of Halacha or tradition as something carved in stone and we have to follow it or ape it.

I've always sensed movement in Halacha. My studies have proven to me wherever we Jews may have lived, we formulated new customs and sometimes those customs differed with the accepted norm of Jewish behavior. For example, Ashkenaz Jewry—whose history can be traced to the settlements of Jews in the Rhine Valley and elsewhere in Central Europe—had a different prayer form than the Jews who came from North Africa, the Sephardic community. An example is the eating of rice on *Pesach* (Passover). The rabbis had arrived at an understanding of what are the forbidden grains known as *hametz* (leavening). The Sephardic Jews said rice is a staple and it's not like the grains forbidden by the rabbis.

So if you attend a *seder* at a Sephardic home, you will be given a dish of lamb and of rice.

The Ashkenaz Jews also refused to allow lamb on the seder plate. It reminded them of the lamb that was brought as an offering in the temple. Yet, if you pay close attention to the oldest traditions, lamb was welcome at the Pesach seder.

We can go on and on. Jewish life is a Halacha, a journey, a never-ending journey. Our tradition never condemns anyone to perdition or purgatory. Return, repentance, *Teshuvah* is extended to everyone. That's the meaning of Yom Kippur, the day of atonement. No matter what serious sin you may have committed, there is always the possibility of return to the community.

We differ from the other traditions prevalent in this world. We refuse to condemn anyone forever. We reject the Christian notion that in Adam's fall, we all fall. Adam is responsible for his personal deeds or misdeeds; the same is true for everyone else. In the fifth commandment, we find the text, "sins of the parents will be born by the children." The prophet, Ezekial, interprets this text. He says no one carries the sin of his or her parent. The activity of the parent may have impressed itself so that in the next few generations, remembrances of the misdeed may be told and retold and perhaps even imitated. But the later generations also have the possibility of changing the "family personality." We have many extant cases proving this point.

Thanks to the new science of psychology, the sources of behavior are discoverable. If you recall the movie, *The Godfather*, at least one or two descendants of the arch leader of the Mafia family turned a corner and became respected, honorable, non-violent members of society. It's true some laughed at them and said, "They don't have the guts to do what we did." Yet, they were able to break their attachments, physical and otherwise, and follow a different path.

In Jewish folklore, there is a saying, "Keep your distance. Don't get too close to the repentant one." Why? The odor is overwhelming. I think we've outgrown this form of thinking. We who have accepted the lessons of the sciences are saying that each one of us, in our own way, shapes our destiny. God is involved, but we are the actors.

No one can shake history. It leaves its indelible mark, sometimes in our bodies and sometimes in our psyche. Part of the journey is to find the invisible cord that ties you to the past, and we must try to fathom what the past is trying to say. The past is not a prisoner. The past is the platform upon which we stand. I cannot come along and say that the medicine practiced, for instance, in the Talmud has a special worth; and yet, no matter what it may be, we owe it a sense of allegiance.

Even though it is part of the sacred past, it has a vote and not a veto. In other words, we give it honor, we study it, we try to compare it to our current level of scientific knowledge. We say to ourselves that the human has always been in a state of becoming, forever discovering the hidden, the forgotten, the implied. The human never stops in his or her search for the essence, the truth, the ultimate.

Many years ago in the Rhine Valley, great teachers of the rabbinic lore lived and taught.

They were aware of the surrounding world. They were cognizant of the findings of the great thinkers. But they didn't live under a forbidding cloud, a church, an ecclesia that dictated what was legitimate and what was forbidden. They were open to all that nature had to teach. They were aware of the power of vegetation. They understood certain herbs and plants had healing power. These herbs and plants, when not used properly, were destructive, claiming many victims. These teachers of whom we speak stood in awe of these products of nature. In Bavel, for instance, we Jews sponsored medical schools. The graduates of these schools eventually came to Europe and brought the findings of the great researchers.

We know, for instance, some of these scholars were also merchants. They brought silk and fine cotton, exceptional wool, and precious stones. They also brought the latest information pertaining to the herbal culture. I, for one, am forever amazed at the sophistication of these people.

To me the telling statement is, *Mikol M'lamdai Hiscalty*, "I have gained wisdom from all of my teachers." Wisdom is not necessarily the private domain of the few, but it is there to be shared far and wide. These scions of learning and investigation never tired in their pursuit of learning. We have many stories of wise men and women who would take walks in the forest or other places and seek and search for seldom-used plants. These wise people knew intuitively what can be of service to the welfare of humans and what is detrimental. No one was ever condemned for searching and questioning. A telling saying was, "Each one of us at the time of our birth is privy to all knowledge." Folklore said that the soul, which was the divine breath possessed by each one of us, is held back. And as Isaac Bashevis Singer once taught us, periodically a soul escapes the *Malach* (guardian) and fulfills its mission of bringing insight and knowledge to the human scene.

Behind this notion lies the concept of *Bashert* (destiny), as if to say each one of us is given an assignment by the Creator. We are expected to discover our destiny and fulfill it. Part of the destiny is a) your life partner; b) the hidden knowledge which you are carrying that can be of use to human kind, c) your assignment for *tikkun olam*, the repair of the world. In order for history to be fulfilled, for the awaited *Mashiach* to arrive, and to experience the peace for which we are always praying—all of this can come about when each one of us discovers the Bashert in his or her life.

I find these days more and more people paying attention to Bashert. It's as if we have come to the conclusion that the world we hope to build, a world based on material goods, is not the ultimate solution for peace.

Once you accept the concept of Bashert, you are bound to seek and find what is there in life that's tying everything together for you. I have spent a lifetime (87 years) trying to understand and to answer, "Why am I here?" I don't believe in pure chance. I do believe in interconnectedness. I will never deny the notion that all of us humans are descendants of an ancient first human, or as we say in Hebrew, *Adam Harishon*.

Over and over again, I experience an ancient dream, finding myself in a distinctive and defined quarter surrounded by mystery, and yet feeling that in this mystery lies the key that will open the closed doors of my existence. I personally feel my destiny urged me to try and peruse the highways and the byways of all that exist. I'm sure it's part of the *Mikol Mlamday Hiscalty*—I've learned from all my teachers, Jew and non-Jew alike. I differ, I know, from many traditional rabbinic authorities who will always tell you, stay away from the writings of *Edom* or *Yishmael*—Christian and Islamic teachings. There are even some who would keep us from studying the wisdom of the East. I differ from them. I believe the urge to know everything is the God-gift. God doesn't want us to look at the human race or the human experience as a collection of little corners and cubicles, but rather to find the cord that ties it all together. Whenever I accept a piece of wisdom from another, I am opening some doors closed to me.

XIII

This morning, I felt insecure. Two days ago, I returned to North Carolina from Maine. All of my Maine goods have been shipped to North Carolina. Thus, I wondered, if the rabbinic saying, *M'shaneh makom, m'shaneh mazal* (change your abode, and your constellation of the stars—mazal—will follow suit) is true?

My *makom*, my new abode, differs slightly from my abode in Maine. There, too, I lived in a complex for older, retired people. There, too, I had questions about myself, my physicality, my hope in my future. But here I sense a new truth. For the first time in my life, I've met American Jews of the southern parts of this country. I've listened to their stories. I've listened to the tales of them being scattered throughout the south. It's not an extant literature. It's almost as if many felt: "Be a decent citizen away from home, and be a true Jewish citizen at home." Is that possible? I think it is.

I think of the famous Coen letter addressed to his family in Germany and in the Carolinas. He taught you must return to that from which you've received.

In this community I find a sense of sharing, of extending oneself, of being honest in all your undertakings. Be proud of your Jewishness. There is no need to hide.

I recall when I was a Yeshiva student in New York. I travelled with my Hebrew books, but I always made sure they had a cover that wouldn't identify them. One day, a man was sitting next to me on the subway train and asked me if my book was written in Japanese. Hebrew wasn't recognized.

Now my daughter, Rina, is teaching Hebrew at a public high school in Guilford County. Every day I meet someone who is ready to share one of his or her secrets with me. More often than not, it's a discovery on their part that they had Jewish ancestors. It seems as if there is a burgeoning feeling of acceptance.

What does this acceptance mean and what does it imply? First of all, I'm also finding more and more mixtures. I'm hearing of non-Jews coming forward in the various towns of North Carolina, meeting with rabbis and, more often than not, going all the way and becoming Jews. I met a man recently who had his DNA traced by supplying the researchers with a blood sample. He discovered that his family's origin was in the northern part of India; yet, there was no trace of ancestors that came from Palestine or Babylonia. It led him to believe, and I agree with him, that during every period we've had people known as the mixed multitude who joined us.

This has been our story from day one. The mixed multitude, according to the Bible, first appeared at the time of the Exodus from Egypt. Again, we read of the mixed multitude in Joshua's time. I venture to guess that, from the earliest days of our existence as a distinct people, there have been inquiries and there have been joiners; and we're seeing it again in our time. It's as if it's part of the divine scheme. After all, the text tells us we will never disappear. Yet, we have had casualties again and again, some of a religious nature, others purely through assimilation. And yet we're still alive. The mixed multitude plays a significant part in our present and future.

Assuming my contention is correct, then the song sung in the various concentration camps, "do not consider this to be the final way," is as true today as it was then. We will never disappear. This is our faith.

XIV

You may legitimately cite the saying in the Talmud, "Don't rely on signs and miracles." There is much to be done by each and every one of us. We all would like to leave our signature or imprint on the monuments of our times. We all would like to say to our progeny, "I was involved in this or in that." Thank God we can.

Take for instance this community in which I am now living. Greensboro, North Carolina. It has a great reputation in American Jewish affairs. Per capita, it is a leading contributor to Jewish causes, if not the leading one. We take our Jewishness seriously. We want to survive. And so, we are bubbling with programs. Summer programs, annual visits to places of Jewish significance, trips to Israel, etc. None of this happens by chance. Many sleeves are rolled up. Much energy is used and discharged in all of these programs. Young and old are involved.

In our community, there is an interesting therapist who does soul work. She contends souls never cease to exist. There's a level of existence prior to birth and another post mortem. I've spent many hours with her and I'm amazed how close I am to her in my thinking. In my many years of therapy with Freudian and Jungian analysts, the issue of an energy level beyond that which is known to our senses plays an important role. As if to say, no time is the final time. Everything is in a state of becoming.

These days, that feeling grows in me. I am convinced that the economic meltdown of the last few years was nature catching up with us and saying we have not been the good guardians of life. We have not taken seriously the Creator's message: "Now you are a living being. Go out and take care of the world." If anything, we've molested the world. We've torn up acres and acres of land, we've destroyed trees, we've polluted waters, we've filled the atmosphere with all sorts of carbons thinking that this is progress. And along comes nature and says, No, it's not. Progress is when you discover who you really are and the message you have been carrying. What is your assigned task in the healing of the world?

We can't avoid this question because it's the very nature of our being: the task and the assignment of taking care of the world. I am not taking care of the world when I selfishly insist so much belongs to me and I want even more. The Ethics of the Fathers asked, "Who is the wealthy one?" And their answer was, "He who is happy with his life and being." In other words, he doesn't keep on asking for more and more and more. The happy one is that person who researches himself or herself and finds his or her latent powers—then takes them and shares them with others.

To watch a friend, a companion, a student smile and convey the feeling of "Aha! I get it!" is beyond description. It's the height of achievement. We are all asked to be messengers, or better still, companions in the search for true meaning in life. The Ethics of the Fathers advises us to acquire for ourselves companions, people who study together, people who act together, people who consider the problems of the world together. The sages actually said when two people gather together for sacred purposes, there is a third companion, namely the Spirit of God.

All of us must listen to the urging of the Creator. All of us are faced with the task of being the caretakers of the world. We come into this life with an inner plan. We spend our lives tracking that inner plan, bringing it to consciousness, and being guided by it.

I'm convinced that in my case, the ups and downs of my life were all part of the plan. At times, I'm sure, I was the good steward. At other times, I was poking in the corners of the darkness. Fortunately, there was enough *Ego* in me that overcame the possibilities of my *Yetzer Harah*, my not-so-good inclinations.

I know when I'm in a state of negative-acting, shadow-acting, another side of me pulls me back. I feel as if a new door has been opened. As if a closed place is now allowing me to come in and learn from it.

I know in my inner soul that I will conquer new heights. I'm grateful to God for having lived the life I have lived. I express my thanks for the many opportunities presented to me and in which I've succeeded in doing God's work. I also thank God for letting me learn on my own the dangers of "poking about" in the corners of the shadow. I've always felt that in the chaos that's life, seeds are to be found for new and interesting developments. We are always in a state of becoming; we are never in a state of arrival.

For all of this I thank God. To me, God is not a being; but God is the eternal force that existed prior to creation and will continue ad infinitum.

I attended a luncheon recently and this very topic was discussed. Not formally, but tablemates speaking to one another. I ventured the notion that we are all in a state of becoming; and therefore, the saying of the rabbis, just as you thank God for the good, so should you thank him for the not so good. Both can be your teachers. I deeply believe this. It's the engine that drives me and keeps me going in life. There were times when I was ready and prepared to throw in the towel. There were days when I said, "enough already." But somehow another voice took over and, on its heels, a new opportunity, a new door appeared.

Recently I had a conversation with Rabbi Eliezer Havivi who I consider to be one of American Jewry's great heroes. He's always respected me and sees me as a survivor of many years in the rabbinate, for which I am grateful. In this conversation, we spoke about fellow Jews who, because of circumstances and age, are living in retirement homes, very few among the many. And to the native population of these retirement places, they represent "the Jew," or better still, an example of what it means to be a Jew. They are bombarded with questions. Their questioners seem to assume that they are in possession of all the mystique that one hears about Jews in non-Jewish circles.

So the rabbi and I discussed the possibility of coming up with a book or pamphlet which might be entitled, *Some Answers When Questions are Asked.* My daughter and I hope to author such a book and make it available to anyone who is seeking basic answers.

Many years ago, I taught a course at OLLI (Osher Lifelong Learning Institutes) on basic Judaism. Some of my former students have written to me and asked that I gather together my notes and come out with a book called, *Basic Judaism*. It won't have that title but it will, I hope, fulfill that request. Many of our fellow Jews have been blessed with knowledge and skill and have managed to become leaders in their respective fields of endeavor. But, many of them have said to me, "Rabbi, I am a recipient of advanced degrees and titles; yet, in my Judaism, I'm no more than Bar Mitzvah-plus."

One of my friends has suggested that we establish Salons for the purpose of further study. You see, we Jews have been around for thousands of years. Our contributions to western and eastern culture have been legion. We are proud of this fact. But how many of us have taken the time to search and research so that we might boast of proficiency in our

Jewishness equal to our proficiency in more secular undertakings.

I plan to devote the rest of my life to the Salon movement. I see my Jewishness as a great banquet, in fact a smorgasbord. We are rational and we are mystical. We are of this world and the worlds yet to come. The Jews who lived in Spain studied Aristotle and the other great minds of western culture never neglecting the Talmud. The Jews of Europe centered their learning mostly on what the Talmud had to say. And when the two met, there was an exchange of culture between those of the Iberian Peninsula and those of the Rhine Valley.

For most of us, the dominant method of Jewish learning and Jewish living stemmed from the Rhine Valley. We were, by choice, *Ashkenazi Jews*. The great shaper of Ashkenazi thought was *Rashi*. In fact, I would recommend that everyone read the trilogy, *Rashi's Daughters*. You will find in that trilogy all and everything that separates us from the rest of the world and all and everything that ties us to it.

I will never cease in my wondering why Jews survived as a people when so many other communities disappeared. We've had our casualties, it's true, but our sacred texts, i.e., the Torah and the prophets and the writings, told us again and again we will always be a minority; and yet, our influence will reach far and wide. How true. As early as the eighth century BCE, the Jewish commonwealth of "The Land of Israel" was challenged by its neighboring powers. Egypt, Assyria, and later Babylonia constantly threatened us. King Solomon died, and the country split into the southern and the northern lands of our people. Before long, incursions occurred and our people were carried off into captivity.

We survived. Some in a hidden way. Some in outward defiance. We survived. We said to ourselves, "Netzach Yisrael," the eternity that is Israel will never be denied. It's us.

Many have asked me: "Were the sacrifices of the past centuries and generations worth it?" Yes. Never say this is the final road. Our spirits continue after our demise; our life continues, too. Even with death there is a state of becoming. That's why we continue to believe the road which we are traversing is never the final road.

If I believe in an unfolding, never-ending future, I see the past with all of its shortcomings as one of the many roads I was destined to follow. Each one of us is forever asking, "who are we?" We never really know. We are always in a state of unfolding and becoming. The beauty of life lies in its mystery, in the unexpected. When we were young, we thought one way. As we grew older, our thoughts changed. All stages are legitimate, and all are to be expected. None of us enter into life as finished products.

Many times I personally feel I've missed the boat. I could have, I should have, I might have behaved one way or another. But that was yesterday. I can't change it. I can only say: Thank God for the opportunities of the days gone by. They provoked in me an interest in what was yet to be and a hope and a yearning that I will be there to accept it.

When I was young, before I learned how to read, I drew energy from my father's stories.

Some came from our sacred writings and some were tales of his youth. My father had an aggressive streak. He was convinced the way he followed, based on his Talmudic learning, was the way for him as a person and as a Jew. It never occurred to him that we, his children, might choose other paths, or that even his wife saw life in a different way. Because of it, I just acted. I aped. I seldom questioned and experimented.

At the age of three, my father taught me how to read Hebrew. By the age of four, I was reading the books, mostly in Hebrew, given to me by my father.

My mother approached life in a lighter vein. She was a beautiful woman, very modish in her dress, and quite familiar with the ways of the world. In fact, at the age of four, she taught me how to play cards—casino. My father was opposed to such frivolous activities. In his case, the sole purpose in life was the mastering of the rabbinic texts.

Almost by the process of osmosis, I absorbed these texts. I seldom spent much time on the codes, the do's and don't's of Jewish life and lore. In fact, many times when I was taught a new law, I found a way around it. My genius became, even at an early age, to find the loopholes which each law produced. This, of course, didn't sit well with my father; but eventually he did admit that, unlike my brother, I sought the whys and wherefores of these laws. My brother, who later became a mathematician, meticulously observed the rules themselves. At the Yeshivot I attended and at the seminary where I received my ordination as a rabbi, I was known as the one who was always asking, "Why?"

I knew deep inside of me that I was under a protective cloud. I felt very close to Hashem and always sought the means for finding favor in Hashem's eyes. I thought what Hashem wanted of me, I was ready to do; but what "the spokesman" of Hashem wanted of me, I always questioned.

I'm still that way. I don't think anything in this life is carved in stone.

XV

In the Book of Psalms, we read, if God is not the builder or the architect of a project, it will never succeed. The God aspect is the eternal aspect of life, that which never ends, that which has been in existence since the moment of creation. Many times we feel that God seems to be out of our affairs. Some people say he's never a resident landlord, but rather an absentee landlord. They assume that God is so entangled in everything that happens in this world. They say, on the other hand, you can't expect to be so knowledgeable of all that is yet to be.

What does this mean? What do we mean by God being the builder or the architect, the One who is always present? Is God the puppeteer? Does He pull the strings? And we the puppets respond to the puppeteer's commands? Not according to the rabbis. They teach us that we are people of choice. We're forever acting, responding to the eternal voice that's within us.

My mentor and seminary professor, Mordecai Kaplan, once said, "A scientist in the laboratory who discovers something new is only unfolding that which has always been there." He called those instances *God moments*. He said at that moment, God is the power that makes for salvation. God is there, not acting, but rearranging the current order of things.

You see, from this point of view, God is the cook. We are the preparers. We present the final dish.

I never feel alone in this world. I may feel estranged, but not alone. I may feel I'm not part of the crowd, but not alone. I may feel that the journey on which I've embarked is not every man's journey, but I'm not an outcast because of it. If anything, I am doing God's work by creating and forming and preparing another dish.

About five or six years ago, I told my friends, "The congregation in which I am currently involved, Etz Chayim Synagogue of Portland,

Maine, is a gathering place for Jews without boundaries." By that I meant people affirm they are Jews, acknowledge it, espouse it, but don't feel their Jewishness is dependent on someone's code. If anything, all codes are open to chance acknowledgements. I act because there is a voice inside of me that brings me to the act. I resist because there is a counter voice that suggests to me perhaps I should sit back and see if there are any other choices for whatever I want to do. And not being bound is a driving aspect. Not being bound.

My orthodox friends feel all of life is a binding process. In the morning when you pray, you are bound by the *tefillin* straps. When you eat, you are bound by the rules of *Kashrut*. In the intimate aspects of life, you are bound by the periodic responses of the body.

Those of us who are not in the orthodox camp and are saying everything is in a fluid state of becoming rather than a static state of *so it is written* turn to the world and say, "Since we are not static people, we can always speak in terms of possibilities."

I was born in 1924. The world was still in a state of becoming. The First World War was fought with the rationale, "It's the war to end all wars." By 1929, when the great crash occurred, we weren't sure. The war was over, but despair, discouragement, and hopelessness were rampant. They opened the way for the autocratic regimes, the Nazis, the fascists, the communists, Franco's Spain, and Hirohito's Japan.

The world didn't settle down until 1945. Even then, the evil that produced these right-wing governments continued. What did it teach us? The evil that springs forth every so often in the breast of humans is as old as life itself. The first two brothers, Cain and Abel, fought each other. Cain killed Abel. After the flood story, God says, I will not destroy the world. I know the human is not divine. The human spends his life trying to find the key to the door that will cleanse him of his evil and infuse him with the goodness that exists in this world.

We have to live with faith and with hope; otherwise, the battle is lost. We have to say, despite everything, don't give up. Keep on trying. Keep on changing. Keep on fighting. Keep on believing. Who shall lead us? "Who shall guide us," the prophet asks. We have the answers. We just ignore them. Every one of us knows that at some point in life, there is a guiding force within him or herself that can lead him or her to a land more promising than the one in which we're living. Underneath all the rot, a beautiful future awaits us.

So, we go on from day to day and say, "Thank you, God, for restoring my soul, for giving me a chance to try again." When the day is over and we review it, we will usually find some of our activities weren't of the best. We say to ourselves that we are potential heroes or potential scoundrels. If we're fortunate, we don't let ourselves be entrapped by any scandalous activity and say, "I won't go there. That's not for me. That's a foolish road. I'll take another turn and hope and pray the choice was right."

So, my friends, take up the torch, wave the flag, stand at the street corner, and urge all passers-by to look both ways before deciding on the future path. There are always choices, there are always opportunities, just have faith.

XVI

We humans are challenged every day of our lives. When our eyes open up just fresh from dreamland, an inner message is waiting for our response. This message may call on us to act in some way or another, perhaps courageously, perhaps ordinarily. The message hopes that it can be added to the collection that we call *Tikkun Haolom*, the healing of the World, or the healing of the Universe. Remember, we take the notion of healing seriously, whether it be the healing of the body, the mind, or the spirit. That being the case, we must continue to see ourselves as Hashem-appointees, better known as angels.

In our Jewish liturgy, the notion of angels appears again and again, as if to say Hashem has surrounded Himself with an army, call them angels, call them seraphim, or any other name, whose sole task in life is to carry out what Hashem feels is necessary to keep the Universe in a state of preparedness. These creatures of whom we speak, according to our thinking, may not even know their assignment. They may ignore it. They may shrug their shoulders and act as if this is just some silly nonsense. But it isn't so. Our tradition has told us that Hashem will never bring the world to its proper state by Himself.

In Genesis, Hashem states, "Let us create one who is like us." In other words, the human, for all practical purposes, is an extension of Hashem Himself. Hashem does not call for intermediaries. He does call for helpers. He does call for beings who understand and fathom the world of which Hashem speaks. One must note that in this world, in Hashem's world, goodness is uppermost. If its opposite appears, it's not the act of an ordinary human. It's the act of one who seeks to undermine all that Hashem wants for this world. Such beings do not support the program of *Tikkun Olam*. They don't feel bound to any call asking for the repair of the Universe. In fact, they derive great pleasure in chaos, in destruction, in the undermining of all that is productive in this world.

This cadre has taken upon itself a program of destruction rather than of repair. It is their hope and wish that all supports, programs, attitudes, and directions that lead to *Tikkun* will fail. They see their task as the destruction of the Universe. Many of them are the Universe's plunderers, people who have dug endless craters throughout this planet and have never filled nor repaired them. They have polluted our waterways in their endless search for fossil fuel. They have brought the food chain to dangerous levels by trying to keep things going, not the way Nature would have it, but bottom-line directed. They feel love is a waste of time. Instead of saying, "The model for behavior is the One who keeps all of its creative passions and juices focused and in tow," they say, "Who is the hero?" and answer "The one who never says 'no' to anything; nor does he ever encourage that which calls for encouraging."

We have recently experienced a terrible economic meltdown. The culprits are people who refuse to live by any approach which would limit their wildest dreams. Many of them said, "The world is our playground, and we are free to do with it as we see fit. Forget the victims who stand in our way. Forget the lonely, the forgotten, the sickly, the abandoned. They are the dregs of humanity—let's eliminate them."

The teachers of German National Socialism spoke that way. No room for the handicapped, no room for the helpless, no room for the minorities. They were housed in the concentration camps.

We believe in *Tikkun Olam*. We feel all life is potentially good. We urge ourselves and others to ask the constant question: What can we do to mend the rips in the fabric of our world? To us, the concept of *mitzvah* addresses this issue. What is a *mitzvah*? When we say Hashem sanctified us by giving us an opportunity to mend the otherwise broken Universe—that's a *mitzvah*. Our sages taught one should attempt to perform one hundred *mitzvot* per day.

In my younger years, I knew fellow Yahiva students who walked around with bags of candy asking people to recite a blessing so that they could say, "amen." Two mitzvot for the price of one.

When I was young, I knew Hashem in a very personal way. I spoke to Him. I sought His support. I yearned for His encouragement. When I felt distraught, sad, or anxious, I would recite a prayer. I felt someone heard me. I didn't feel the same way about people. Many times in low moments, many of my friends would try to make light of it. "Oh, come on. You can do better. Oh, come on, it's not as bad as it sounds. Oh come on. There is a way out. You'll find it." That was friend-talk. It reminded me of Job's friends who tried to assure him in his most dark and lonely moments, "Oh, come on. You'll work your way out of it." Job knew he could never do it by himself. And he didn't return to his love of life until he felt Hashem was in the middle of it all.

There's a wonderful passage in Job when Hashem asks Job, "Were you there? Where were you at the moment of Creation? Why do you expect that which is hidden to so many is open to you? A time will come when you will find yourself again, but that time is not of your doing. It's of Hashem's doing."

So what shall we do? What shall we say? I personally feel that no system has all the answers. I think Hashem has revealed Himself to all of us. Some of us are more discerning than others. We have answers foreign to many of our friends.

I don't feel the only way to Hashem is the established way. I think Hashem peeks out of many corners, signaling to us. Sometimes we recognize the signals; other times, they pass us by. I, for one, have found Hashem in the strangest places—in the straight path, in the nooks and the crannies of foreign territories. Sometimes Hashem speaks to me directly, sometimes symbolically. Sometimes He lets me stew for a while wondering where the answer might be.

Never will I say Hashem is dead, Hashem doesn't exist, faith is a figment of our imagination. To me, Hashem is as real as the nose on my face. I can't describe His appearance, but I can describe His energy. And I feel blessed in this ability. It keeps me alive and gives me the hope I constantly seek. I worry about the world as would any person sensitive to all we hear and read.

I'm reminded of a story. During the terrible days of the Spanish Inquisition, some Jews left Spain under duress. A family of exiles was on a boat and was thrown overboard. They were prevented from reaching a safe harbor. They swam to a lonely island in the middle of the sea. They were left without food or water. Slowly, the members of this family of four began to lose their energy. A young child died; then its sister; then its mother. And finally, the father of the group looked to all sides and said, "Hashem, I know you're here. No matter what may happen to me, I won't give up my belief in You. Perhaps my sad story will move others and someone will be saved."

I can never give up the idea that I'm in this world, assigned to its continuation and upkeep. It's as if someone gave me the tools needed to mend and restore an injured part of our Universe. I can't stop. I know till my dying day, I will feel where the tears and the rips occur, and I will be called to assist in the mending.

It's a tall order. In fact, it seems to have the overtones of arrogance. Why am I special? Why do I think that I can succeed where others have failed? Where will I draw the energy needed to act as a mender in this torn world? I feel we are here as Hashem's assistants. What was said to the first human is being said to me. Now you are a living being. Go take care of the world.

How do you know if you are fulfilling that command or suggestion? What standards do you use? How do you judge? How can you say, "Yes, this is mending. This is tearing." First, let me suggest that the mender prepares the ground for further achievements. The mender never dismisses a problem. If a problem prevails, the mender knows from deep within himself the image of the mended part—as if *Bezalel*, the great builder of the *Mishkan*, has shared his soul with the rest of us. That soul says to us, never say it can't be done. It awaits your energy.

A JEWISH DIALECTIC / 175

When we Jews speak of energy, we bear in mind a term from the earliest days of Jewish experience. The term is, *Kavanah* (intent). We ask ourselves how are we facing our problems? What are our intentions? Do we want to push them aside, or are we ready to address them and heal them? So often in communal affairs, we Jews seem to follow the "push it aside" approach. Again and again, Jewish adults have said to me: In my religious school days intent was never discussed. I was told this is the rule, and so shall ye behave.

Few of us think that way these days. Most of us say Kavanah (intent) is the key. If your Kavanah is honest, and you are truly interested in addressing the problems of the day, then you will find solutions. But if it's to "get it off the table," you will not succeed.

Kavanah calls for honesty and integrity. It has no room for cover up.

Among the Hasidim, it was customary to recite a Kavanah before performing a mitzvah. Usually the formula read, "At this moment, I am prepared and ready to fulfill this mitzvah. May my intents be pure, honest, and stem from my heart. I hope by the mitzvah and its performance my tie to Hashem will be strengthened."

Now, it's true, that many people recited a Kavanah and did not realize a favorable outcome for the said mitzvah or act. If that happened, then we were instructed to go back, meditate, concentrate, ask ourselves questions. Why are things the way they are?

Life has taught us the meditative moment oft times is of greater worth than many medical formulas. In the meditative moment, I abstract myself from the present situation, and I find the freedom to act as the mitzvah would have me act. To use a term of the vernacular, the meditative moment is the shot in the arm that I yearn for.

The meditative moment refreshes you. It helps clear the sense of the clouded life. The moment restores to us all blocked visions so that we can say, "Aha! Now I know what to do and where to go."

Therefore, I suggest that prayer in our times must be more than the printed word in the printed book. Prayer can no longer be the repetition of established formulas. Prayer is the vibrant engagement with powers and forces above and beyond ourselves.

XVII

When I engage in prayer, I'm engaging in conversation with a force that is in me and beyond me. As you know by now, I take seriously the story of Creation. I believe Hashem said, "Now you are a living being. Go take care of the world." I also believe the foreword to this story: Hashem was lonely and sought a partner in the caring of his newly created world.

The entire Creation story is filled with possibilities and suggestions. Eve, the first human's partner, was flesh of his flesh and blood of his blood except for his physiognomy, as if to say that all that was needed for the creation and the survival of the human—the co-partner and co-caretaker of the Universe—was spelled out in Adam.

It's incumbent upon all of us to ask ourselves the question, "Does this apply to me, too?" Perhaps I'm liberated and I don't feel attached to this ancient past. Where does it lead me? In my view, I would say, your voice, dear human, can't be separated from the rest. If you choose to separate yourself, then you're opening up a "new can of beans." You're seeking a new peck of troubles. I can't separate myself physically from my parents; nor could they separate themselves from their family. As Koheleth—Ecclesiastes—said, generations come and generations go, but the world continues on its own path, its own way.

Lately, I've been blessed with interesting dreams. For the past few weeks, a woman has appeared in my dreams. She sits in my chair, faces me, and I feel she's gently trying to guide me along. Whenever I see her in my dream, that night I have a full night's sleep. Last night was one of those nights; and the day that followed was so alive and so meaningful and so creative. I wondered why.

Later that day, some new friends invited me to lead a group in the study of Psalms. The Psalms is a teaching of faith. I think that's a good sign. The world is in a state of turmoil, not knowing where to go. So many feel that might makes right and deny the saying in Scripture, "Not by might, nor with weapons, shall you succeed, but by my Spirit, says Hashem."

I believe fully in that statement. I've travelled both roads. There have been times when I've tried the power play to achieve my goals. There have been other times when I've tried the road of negotiation saying, "Here's where I stand. My adversary has taken another position. But thank Hashem we have reached a state of trust which allows us to seek working solutions."

If I have reached a mature state in any place or aspect, the willingness to give and take has led me forward.

The lady who appears in my dreams seems to imply quietness, acceptance, a willingness to pay attention to another point of view. She seems to say to me, "Hashem has many voices. Hashem has told us more than once, I will listen to the prayers of all who approach me. I don't insist on special documents or special gifts. All are welcome."

This morning at a study session, we realized that within the Jewish community, we have many non-blood relatives. To be a Jew, you don't have to possess only one bloodline. In fact, DNA studies have proven to us that the concept of "the mixed multitude" is real. Many of us are descendants, not necessarily of Jacob's twelve sons, or better, Jacob's thirteen children. From the days of Abraham up to present times, we have always said to those who spoke to us, "Come join us. You are welcome no matter what your origin may be."

Because of this open-mindedness, we have succeeded in enriching the Jewish presence. In Biblical days we were told, "Welcome the stranger. Remember you were strangers in the land of Egypt. Never turn the stranger away." I, for one, am always attuned to the person who comes and shares with me his or her personal history, the one who comes to me and tells me of a long-forgotten Jewish ancestor and feeling that he or she is drawn to the Jewish community.

A day doesn't go by without a discovery.

What does this tell us? Again, I raise the question, where do we go from here? I propose the following:

As Jews, we must live in the day in which we find ourselves. Every day is an opportunity for *Tikkun Olam*, the healing of the world.

Be forever accepting, always saying here's an opportunity. Let's go with it.

Every moment is mitzvah time. Every moment says to you, here I am! Asking, am I helping or hindering? Am I concerned about the future of the Universe? The climate? The great weather extremes? The intractable leaders of our times who still believe might is right? What about people? Does their hunger trouble me? Does their unhappiness cast a pall over me?

What am I doing in the political arena? Am I insisting on the integrity of our political leaders? What am I saying about the buying of votes? What am I saying to those who speak one way and act in another?

Have I reached the point where I can truthfully and honestly say: This I believe. Here I stand.

When you live Jewishly, you affirm there is a way that is the Jewish way. We give that way the title, *Halacha*. Some people see it in monolithic terms. There is only one *Halacha*, only one way that will legitimately lead you to God. Others say the word, *Halacha*, means journey, and every traveler will tell you his or her safety depends on their roadmap and their cooperative connection to the world as a whole.

Many years ago, I was confronted with the question of choice. I was asking myself, who am I? Or better, what am I? I was old enough to receive many sobriquets, some honorable and some degrading. It took me some time to realize that my road is not necessarily every person's road. My many years spent in deep analysis with various analysts helped me see the uniqueness of my own road and my own choices. Sometimes the choices were the choices of the majority. Other times, they were the choices of the travelers who had taken side roads. Whatever the case may have been, they were my choices. Hashem didn't stand in the way when I made those choices. In fact, at times I felt liberated when I affirmed my own choices.

Was I correct? I'm not sure. My life and my spirit tell me I was. All the books I've read and learned sometimes agree and sometimes disagree with my choices. But in the long run I've learned that Hashem asks of us to be ourselves and be true to ourselves.

XVIII

How can we judge ourselves? What tests do we have to pass? Some authorities will tell you there are many telling marks. For instance, in the Book of Leviticus we read the rules and regulations for *M'tzora*. The word is usually translated *leper*. I'm not sure that's the correct translation. According to some authorities, the *tzaruah* is someone who has humbled himself; and the person who is a M'tzora is so humbled that he is excluded from human society.

Our sages, wondering about this state, came to the conclusion that the one who humbles himself and becomes part of that low estate indulged in the worst of human shortcomings—unproven gossip. In other words, one who is forever demeaning, denouncing, destroying the reputation of another is deserving of exile, at least until he admits to the errors of his ways and takes it upon himself to be part of society and not separate himself by his evil tongue.

Because of the culprit's isolation, his own inner guide will express its dislike for the culprit's behavior by making sure that his skin is covered with telling marks urging people to keep their distance, for he is not worthy of human society.

In this case we would say our inner judge—being an honest judge and sensing the two sides of judgment—has expressed itself by saying its residence-owner has not lived up to the basic premise of "love your neighbor as thyself."

If you find it necessary to put others down, to separate yourself and act in a haughty way as if you were the paragon of virtue, then the moment will arrive when someone will be able to say to you, "Judge not lest you be judged," or better still, "Don't judge your friend until you're standing in his place." It's an example of self-judgment.

A second example of self-judgment was provided by Rabbi Nahman of Bratislava. He urged, especially his younger students, to have a notebook at their bedside; and every day before reciting the bedtime prayers, they were to take an inventory: "I did this or I did that. I'd say to myself I will never do it again; or perhaps say that was a good move. That should be repeated." We are capable of such judgments. The Talmud says a human is the best witness of himself. No one is nearer to me than myself. If I'm honest and willing to accept the judgments I hear in my head, I will be able to ultimately walk on my destined path.

Throughout our entire life, we are sometimes actively, sometimes pensively, on a journey. It's our journey. No one else's but our own. And we are the overseers of our journey. We humans, in all honesty, should say to God, "Thanks for trusting me. Thanks for giving me the right and the privilege of overseeing my journey. Thanks for saying to me no matter what I've done, I can always come back."

A Hasidic story is told of a prince who lived in a royal court. His father, the king, wondered about him. He was wild. No matter whom he met he expected acknowledgement. Forever he would go from town to town, knock on people's doors, identify himself, and ask for "the royal tithe." He seldom specified the tithe. He just said "the tithe." When the homeowner tarried in providing the tithe, the prince and his underling would help themselves to the owner's possessions.

The prince insisted on his immunity. No one can tell him what to do. He had access to all of the regulating channels in the realm. The prince continued in these nefarious activities, acting as if no one will dare question him.

One day, his father, the king, was informed by one of his attendants that the prince was instilling extreme fear in the hearts of the citizens of the realm. The royal father was terribly disturbed. Over the years he had developed a fine reputation. No one would suspect him of entering a private home and helping himself to the owner's possessions. Nor would the king ever insist on a royal tithe. The king believed the recipient of tithes is God Himself and not human satellites, whether they were priests serving in the temples, prophets commenting on the present and the future, or a final voice to be honored, to be heard, and to be obeyed.

The king called for his son. The king expected an immediate response to his order; the prince said, "This will most likely be the last time that he'll speak to me, for I have a plan and that plan will take him from us." He was overheard, and one of his father's loyal subjects told the king about it.

Unlike previous times when the prince, in a moment of rash disobedience, painted pictures implying or urging the demise of the king, this time *he had been heard*. His words were reported. There was no escape route.

One of his, that is the prince's, lackeys warned him of the king's wrath. You better leave, said the lackey. Don't go in to see the king. Your father will never forgive you. The prince quickly gathered his things together, stored them in wagons, and left with his retinue without telling anyone.

The wagons were overflowing with precious possessions—furs, jewelry, spices—all that is needed for an extraordinary, wealthy household. They travelled for many days, avoiding the major highways of the realm. The prince had many loyal followers. He kept them in furs, in funds, in all of the precious goods of his day. The prince had his spies. They would wander off for one or two days at a time and bring back reports from the realm. What are people saying? What are the king's plans? What will happen if the prince is ever caught?

As time went on, the prince's possessions were quickly vanishing. The prince no longer had access to the citizens' precious possessions. If anything, he was aware of the king's order: "If the prince is ever spotted, the authorities are to be informed. The informer will be handsomely rewarded."

One day, the prince came out of his bedroom. He had just experienced a long, sleepless night. He was distraught, his voice was shrill, his hands shook, and it seemed as if he was about to fall. His personal servants ran to his side, and he waved them away. "But Your Highness, we are worried by your demeanor.

What can we do to lessen the terror and sense of hopelessness etched on your face?"

The prince replied, "I feel abandoned and alone. My father refuses to see me. In fact, he has offered a reward to anyone who can find me and bring me to him. What is life if your father refuses to acknowledge you and seeks only to destroy you—as if to say you are the bad seed every father fears. What can I do? I know I have erred. I know I have brought shame to my father. I know I have not been the son I should have been. What shall I do?"

At this moment, his most trusted servant, the one who cared deeply for him, his partner in all of his adventures, said, "Your Highness, I have bad news. Your stocks have diminished, very little food is left, some of your retainers have gone home, and I only envision a dark future for us." The prince cried out, "What shall I do!"

Suddenly, he heard an inner voice say to him, "Send your father a note. Confess and ask for forgiveness. Perhaps he will call you back." The prince, overcome by his despair, uttered a deep, hollow sound. It seemed as if he was ready to give up his life. His trusted friend put his arm around his shoulder, and together they sobbed.

It was a dreary time for the former illustrious prince. Alone, forgotten, exiled from his father's court. Three days later, a messenger arrived. The king said, "I, too, repent for not having concerned myself with your life. I thought that time would be the great teacher, forgetting no one can take the place of a parent in a young person's life. Please come home. Let's try again."

The prince, filled with joy and with hope, prepared himself for the long journey home. He gathered his remaining servants together and shared with them his current dilemma. One servant said, "If I may, I, too, had to find the way to be one with my father. With God's help, the gap was closed and we are one again. It will happen to you, too. When father and son admit their respective shortcomings, God steps in and cements the gaps."

When they arrived at the palace, father and son spoke to each other and were reconciled.

I have always felt this is the life lesson, for I, too, am a father and I had to bridge many places so that my family could be one again.

XIX

It seems to me many of us are estranged from the Father of us all, Hashem Himself. We are too concrete in our understanding of Hashem. We judge Hashem in human terms and expect Hashem to follow human patterns of behavior. Hashem is not a human. He is beyond the human. That's why we try throughout our lives to reach him. Our journey is a journey towards Hashem. When and if we become one with Hashem, then all the shadows and all the dark vibes and all the pain and suffering seem to be set aside. For the source of much of our pain is the great divide that separates us from Hashem Himself.

How do we bridge the chasm, the great divide that separates us from Hashem? We begin by defining for ourselves who Hashem is. I am convinced each of us is the author of his own theology; and if we were to gather in a room, none of us would describe Hashem in equal terms. We may speak of the power of Hashem. We may speak of the possibilities which Hashem brings to us. But who Hashem is? How do we describe him? That's a personal task.

In these my senior years, when the phrase chanted on Yom Kippur, "Cast us not aside in our senior days," becomes poignant, it speaks to me and to other seniors like myself. I know Hashem exists, the One that I speak of, who like the forgiving Father, is willing to say, "Let's try again," and who will never have the bitterness of the Red Queen who shouted, "Off with their heads!"

There are some of you who may say there are passages in our Torah which tell us that for some deeds or misdeeds, we are candidates for capital punishment. What does the Torah mean when it says, "Such is the verdict"? Some of my teachers taught me there are too many details attached to these passages. Yes, the deed is a capital deed; but there must be witnesses who attest the deed took place. It's impossible to find in any court of law witnesses who will completely agree in absolute detail when giving testimony. They bear in mind the "look on the culprit's face," "the culprit's demeanor," "the arguments that led to the capital act." That being the case, how can you ever completely be sure the act was one that deserves capital punishment?

Judaism has always stood on the forgiving side. Well, maybe, who knows, perhaps. In fact, the rabbis said that any court who finds someone guilty of a capital crime and punishes that person once in its lifetime is a court of misdeeds. Judaism always felt the human is by nature a good being. The good is hidden, tucked away somewhere in the deepest recesses of a person's psyche. When it's extracted from its corner and allowed to be its owner's guide, the crassest of sinners will return in an honest way to the human scene.

I personally have great faith in the human. I share the frustrations of many. The day will come, as predicted by the Prophet, when "all of humankind will accept Hashem" the One we worship, the One who loves us, believes in us, trusts us, and knows that ultimately we will be at His side. AMEN.